THE GREEN KNIGHT

GEORGE GASCOIGNE

The Green Knight
Selected Poetry and Prose

edited by Roger Pooley

CARCANET NEW PRESS / MANCHESTER

Introduction and Selection copyright © 1982 by Roger Pooley

All Rights Reserved

First published in 1982 by
CARCANET NEW PRESS LTD
210 Corn Exchange Buildings
Manchester M4 3BQ

Gascoigne, George
The Green knight.—(Fyfield Books)
I. Title   II. Pooley, Roger
828'.309   PR2535

ISBN 0-85635-279-9

*The publisher acknowledges the financial assistance of the
Arts Council of Great Britain*

Printed in England by SRP Ltd., Exeter

CONTENTS

INTRODUCTION

GASCOIGNE's achievement as a writer really ought to be in the *Guinness Book of Records*. He wrote the first treatise on prosody in English, the first sonnet sequence, the first original blank verse poem, the first prose comedy, part of the first version of a Greek tragedy, and a contender for 'the first English novel'. But too often he is taken by literary historians as a merely transitional figure, building on the formal achievements of Wyatt and Surrey, and really only clearing the way for what Sidney, Spenser and Shakespeare were to achieve a few years later. The line on his friend Whetstone's 'Remembrance' of him, 'And we devoured the sweet of all his sweat', can thus be adapted to a description of Gascoigne's place in literary 'progress', rather than its original meaning, that Gascoigne's readers can benefit from his works in their own right. The point of a selection such as this is to persuade readers of poetry that Gascoigne wrote a number of good poems, and a few really superb ones; and that his narrative prose has the zip of immediacy as well as some psychological subtlety. With some of the poems, it certainly helps to know the historical context, but this is a question of seeing Gascoigne's response to real events rather than the state of literary convention a lot of the time. Gascoigne wrote of love and money, war and repentance, in a strong and appealing way; and his creation of 'Gascoigne' was not the least of his literary achievements.

Much of Gascoigne's life is a history of failed enterprises. Some of his best later lyrics—'Gascoigne's Woodmanship' and 'The Green Knight's Farewell to Fancy' in particular—take a wry view of this, and 'Woodmanship' develops the view that failure in some enterprises is a positive guarantee of a man's integrity. For instance, failing to make money out of war:

> It will be long before he hit the vein,
> Whereby he may a richer man be made.
> He cannot climb as other catchers can,
> To lead a charge before himself be led,
> He cannot spoil the simple sakeless man,
> Which is content to feed him with his bread.
> He cannot pinch the painful soldier's pay . . .

But, as he admits, he was ambitious. As with Donne, we feel that repentance and the failure to get preferment are closely allied—not that one invalidates the other, or only successful men would be allowed into the kingdom of heaven. We must remember that, towards the end of his life, Gascoigne translated a tract called 'The Needle's Eye' as part of his *Drum of Doomsday*, and by then he was no rich man.

George Gascoigne was born in or around 1539, son of Sir John Gascoigne, MP and JP in Bedfordshire. Sir John was a Catholic (here we see another parallel with Donne); his wife, Margaret, seems to have shared her husband's rather quarrelsome nature. For instance, Sir John disinherited George on his deathbed, and Margaret took her own sister to court over a gold casting bottle from their father's estate.

The education they gave George is not precisely documented. Prouty's biography (whose authority and usefulness I gratefully acknowledge) suggests that he must have shared lessons with his cousins during his mother's visits to Westmoreland; and then studied under Stephen Nevynson at Trinity College, Cambridge. But these are likely explanations, rather than facts. We can be more certain that he entered Gray's Inn to study law in 1555. After a couple of years his interest waned, and we find him hunting and hawking (and trespassing) in Bedfordshire in 1557, and sitting in Parliament with his father as Burgess for the borough of Bedford. While they were meeting in November 1557, Queen Mary died and Elizabeth succeeded her. Sir John was entitled to be in the procession in the coronation in 1558, but was ill, and so his eldest son George took his place. It was a turning point. He was seduced by the glamorous possibilities of court life, and gave up the law for it.

Being a courtier was expensive. The fine clothes (essential if the young aspirant was to cut a dash) were only part of his prodigal expenditure. There were financial rewards for the successful, such as Christopher Hatton, but Gascoigne missed them. So it may be that his court experience was a source of his astringent poetry about money and the lack of it as well as his grasp of the conventions and courtesies of love.

In November 1561 he married Elizabeth, the widow of William Bretton and mother of the future poet Nicholas. She was also connected by what one document calls 'a false marriage' to Edward Boyes. Disputes with Boyes involved Gascoigne in litigation of various sorts as well as a fight in Redcross Street in London between the two men and their retainers. The poem beginning 'Of all the letters in the Christ's cross row' also derives from this conflict. In the middle of all this, in 1563, Gascoigne was 'cast off' by the court and retired to Willington in Bedford.

Money pressures may have been the main reason for his return to Gray's Inn in 1565. The return is marked by the 'Memories', five poems on themes given him by his friends there; and those sharp, innovative pieces are indicative of how productive from a literary point of view his second spell at Gray's Inn was to be. The students there took their drama seriously. With Francis Kinwelmarshe Gascoigne translated Euripides' *Jocasta* via an Italian version. His version of Ariosto's *Supposes* was written for Gray's Inn too. Many of Gascoigne's early poems seem to be written from within the court ethos, and the ceremony, and the rules of love games and the lover's psychology; but it is during this second period at Gray's Inn that we see his work developing a more reflective, independent and even philosophical cast in the context of an active literary coterie. Kinwelmarshe also contributed to the collaborative anthology *The Paradise of Dainty Devises*, and Alexander Nevile translated Seneca's *Oedipus*. Senior members like Serjeant William Lovelace encouraged younger poets.

But the drain of litigation continued, and by 1567 or 1568 Gascoigne returned to farming in Cardington, though he seems to have been in Walthamstow a lot, and of course in London for the courts. The culmination of his troubles came in 1570, when he was imprisoned for debt.

Both the court and the law had been expensive failures for Gascoigne, as they were for many of his contemporaries. Even farming proved to be hazardous—he had an argument with his mother over the ownership of some sheep—so it was hardly surprising that he should take the opportunity to join Sir Humphrey Gilbert's volunteers in support of William of Orange against the Spaniards in the Netherlands. The extent to which this was a war of liberty against the Spaniards and Popery is distinctly limited in Gascoigne's account. This may be the kind of disillusion we get in Spanish Civil War memoirs, but in fact, Gascoigne seems more influenced by Calvinist attitudes after his trip to Holland than before he went. He did develop a very low opinion of the Dutch, closer to Nashe's chauvinism in *Pierce Pennilesse* than Protestant idealism, partly because of their conduct towards the English volunteers. But most important, he developed a sense of the horror and waste of war, one which takes him away from the official Elizabethan ideology and closer to the radical humanism of Erasmus. Certainly, it was no place to mend his fortunes—in 'The fruits of war' he recalls the one opportunity of spoil, which escaped him because the sailors in his ship were too incompetent to catch the prize.

In the midst of all this he was publishing *A Hundreth Sundrie Flowres*, a collection of prose narrative, drama and poetry. Or at least, a printer was publishing it. There has been some doubt about the authorship of some of the pieces, admittedly from the dubious home of those who think the Earl of Oxford wrote Shakespeare; and the main reason is that Gascoigne appears to have been covering his tracks. There is almost as much of a fictional feel to the letters of introduction to the volume as there is to the fiction of *The Adventures of Master F. J.*, the first piece in the collection. Now, for his anonymous translation of *The Noble Art of Venerie or Hunting* he wrote and signed a commendatory poem, and another under a pseudonym. Gascoigne seems to have enjoyed this game of peek-a-boo with his readers. A gentleman (even, or perhaps especially, one who had been in prison for debt) could not be thought to write directly for money; but all the same, he had been accused of being 'a common rhymer and a deviser of slanderous pasquils against divers persons of great calling'.

The *Flowres* were not published while Gascoigne was still in England. He left fairly quickly after his return, probably because of the continuing debt problem. He had got himself elected Burgess of Midhurst in Sussex, the seat of his friend Viscount Montacute (or Montague), and this enabled him to claim parliamentary immunity from creditors. An anonymous letter to the Privy Council accused him of such a ruse, along with manslaughter, atheism, spying and a few lesser reasons for his not being a satisfactory MP.

This sort of pressure may have caused him to embark for Holland rather hurriedly in March 1573; or it may be that the

10

people he went with, William Herle and Rowland Yorke, meant that he was already part of Walsingham's secret service and thus engaged in that sort of activity until August, when he started fighting again. Despite a sea victory, he was fed up with the Dutch and the standards of discipline in his own unit, and went to the Prince of Orange to get leave and a passport. He stayed at Delft some time without getting quite what he wanted—a result of English dissension more than Dutch meanness—but then the Spanish began to threaten Delft. At this point an affair which Gascoigne had had in The Hague caught up with him; the lady sent him a letter. The Hague was now an enemy town, and suspicions were aroused. The Prince still trusted him, though, particularly as he seems to have been one of the few Englishmen who had stayed, and put him in charge of a 'hoy' to harass Spanish shipping.

On the return of an English force, disaster struck. They were fortifying Valkenburgh when the Spaniards arrived, and fled to Leyden. But the gates were barred against them for fear of a ruse to let the Spaniards in. (There had been plenty of cities betrayed to the Spaniards, though not by the rather insignificant English force, and the Spaniards were not generous in victory.) The English had no alternative but to parley. The soldiers were sent home, but Gascoigne and his fellow-officers were held as Spanish prisoners for four months. Gascoigne had nothing but praise for his captor De Licques, but being held hostage was no joy, and his release in October 1574 took him back to England.

It was not to a hero's welcome. The *Flowres* were objected to as wanton, lascivious and scandalous. A revised version, *The Posies* (1575), with a repentant preface, did not convince the Queen's Commissioners and that, too, was seized. But in the two years following, Gascoigne's repentance was substantiated in a whole series of works, all of them in different ways in the *contemptus mundi* tradition—the 'prodigal son' play *The Glass of Government*, the satire *The Steel Glass*, a translation of three religious tracts, *The Drum of Doomsday*, a temperance tract, *A Delicate Diet for Dainty-Mouthed Drunkards*, and various occasional verses.

In August 1576 he was employed by the government to observe affairs in the Low Countries. He went to Paris, and then to Antwerp, where he was an eyewitness of the Spanish

11

sack of the city, recounted in the pamphlet *The Spoil of Antwerp*. He returned in November, and was paid. He prepared *The Grief of Joy*, an imitation of Petrarch, as a New Year's gift for the Queen. Success at last—he was in royal service, he had noble friends and patrons. But he was not well. He died at Stamford, at the home of his friend and admirer George Whetstone, in October 1577.

By no means all of Gascoigne's poems can be slotted into a 'Life and Letters' biography. More than many in this pre-Romantic period, his poems describe a life; but then many are occasional, written for friends, or on their behalf, or within a fictional framework.

The tension between poetry as a witty game and poetry as an expression of felt inner truth is clearest in Gascoigne's love poetry. The exchange between him and a gentlewoman, and the more elaborate ruses in *The Adventures of Master F. J.*, are not the spontaneous overflow of powerful feelings, but their expression within a court culture where the political and economic contract of marriage and the expression of love rarely coincided. Gascoigne was often content to play a few variations on the given tunes; so, for instance, 'Gascoigne's Arraignment' uses a similar dramatic situation to Petrarch's canzone 'Quell' antiquo mio dolce empio', translated by Wyatt as 'Mine old dear enemy, my froward master . . .'. This is distinctly second-rate Wyatt the translator, whereas Gascoigne is at the peak of his more flippant manner, so the comparison is unfair in isolation. But notice how Gascoigne pulls in the morality play cast—Craft the Cryer, Jealous the Jailor and so on—where Wyatt is content to follow the abstractions of his original, and as a result defuses the drama of the situation. Elsewhere Gascoigne might make a great deal too much of the desperate pain of the unrequited lover; but here he uses short lines, bouncy rhythms, and a straightforward vocabulary largely shorn of the technical terms of courtly love. The result is that his real ability to tell a story directly and wittily (as so often, against himself) comes through. The conclusion—'Thus am I Beauty's bounden thrall,/At her command when she doth call'—is the end of a fable as much as a gesture in the courtly tradition. The Englishness, a kind of folk Englishness, of the characters, is the main reason; but it's a structural matter too. Here is a simple story which explains how the current state of affairs came to be. Myth is too grand a word —it's a little personal fable.

The game element in Gascoigne's poetry is not simply in the Italian 'love debate' tradition that surfaces here, and most obviously in *Master F. J.*; it is linked with his being an 'occasional', non-professional poet; the artifice of the poem is its value, its inventiveness rather than its sentiments. The originality—the invention or conceit behind it—is what drives the poem, as, for instance, with the wittily lascivious poem in praise of a woman called Philip who is transformed into a lively sparrow. It's different with resentment: Gascoigne has a firmer, more transparent style in rejection, and the moral indignation can be brought into play in the wake of loss.

Even more successful than this is Gascoigne's very individual satirical vein. William Wallace, the editor of *The Steel Glass*, contrasts that poem with the satires of the 1590s (Donne, Marston, Jonson et al.) by saying that Gascoigne is able to direct his charge of inadequacy against himself as well as against his targets in society at large. True enough; but that doesn't make *The Steel Glass* a very successful poem. The first original blank verse poem in English it may be, but the analysis, impeccably moral as it is, is not very interesting. Gascoigne ties himself very early to the feudal analysis of society into the four estates, and the general line that people should do their jobs within their stated limits has a limiting effect on his imagination. Where the poem is interesting, I think, is in the opening section where he sees his own role as poet in the legend of Philomele (the poem was originally published in tandem with his version of it, a fine balladic sweep too long for inclusion in this selection).

Gascoigne's satirical vein works best when he is involved, when he is satirizing the faults of society from the recognition of his own misfortunes, to which he himself has also contributed, as Wallace suggests; but allied to the directness of personal experience expressed through narrative, his most consistent skill. The poetry about his experiences in the Low Countries has this kind of directness. 'The fruits of war' has a rambling structure; much of the first half is a meditation on the adage 'war is sweet to those who've not tried it' at a rather abstract level, the level which *The Steel Glass* never really leaves. But then Gascoigne plunges into direct narrative, and the nature of his poetic achievement changes from the ordinary to the impressive. This part of the poem, read alongside the prose description of the later spoil of Antwerp, gives an account of war at the sharp end which is difficult to find bettered until our own century. That poignant combination of suffering and muddle which comes through practically every account of the First World War is matched in Gascoigne's writing by his disillusion as he sees that wealth and honour are denied him by incompetence and politicking. Earlier in his career Gascoigne may have felt that the world owed him a living; now his perceptions are unlikely to lead him into poetic whining. He and his fellow soldiers on the brink of shipwreck might be comforted by psalms and prayers, but they soon discover that they're not fighting in a crusade as far as the natives are concerned, and he makes Lord Grey, his Puritan patron, aware of the fact:

> Now ply thee pen, and paint the foul despite
> Of drunken Dutchmen standing there even still,
> For whom we came in their cause for to fight,
> For whom we came their state for to defend,
> For whom we came as friends to grieve their foes,
> They who disdained (in this distress) to lend
> One helping boat for to assuage our woes.
>
> ('Gascoigne's voyage into Holland *an*. 1572')

This poem's twin strengths—narrative excitement and vigorous abuse—are both results of Gascoigne's clear use of his own personality, as a contrast to the villainy of all foreigners (with the exception of his Spanish captor De Licques) and as a victim of circumstances and his own naivety. In some ways it is a rather hard personality with a tendency towards cynicism, but tempered with a winning skill at telling stories against himself. It is at this stage that the 'Green Knight' takes poetic shape.

In the modern fashion I have tended to praise specificity and personality over generality; but it was Gascoigne's handling of truisms that stimulated Yvor Winters to call him one of the six or seven greatest lyric poets of the sixteenth century. It is connected with Winters's characterization of the virtues

14

of the plain style that he wants to set against Petrarchan style, which in his view has been over-valued in histories of Renaissance poetry.

> A theme usually broad, simple, and obvious, even tending toward the proverbial, but usually a theme of some importance, humanly speaking; a feeling restrained to the minimum required by the subject; a rhetoric restrained to a similar minimum, the poet being interested in his rhetoric as a means of stating his matter as economically as possible, and not, as are the Petrarchans, in the pleasures of rhetoric for its own sake . . . The wisdom of poetry of this kind lies not in the acceptance of a truism, at least formally, but in the realisation of the truth of the truism; the realisation resides in the feeling, the style. Only a master of style can deal in a plain manner with obvious matter . . . a poetry which permits itself originality, that is, the breath of life, only in the most restrained subtleties of diction and cadence, but which by virtue of those subtleties inspires its universals with their full value as experience.
>
> (*Forms of Discovery* pp. 3-4)

This is an interesting and influential attempt to make a case for Renaissance sententiousness to a poetry audience raised on Romantic notions of sincerity (and their modernist son, the 'objective correlative'). As such, it is particularly apt for a poet like Gascoigne who explicitly makes his poetry out of his personality, yet within the humanist frame of argument and respect (if not reverence) for the texts and wisdom of the past.

We can see best what Winters is saying by reading 'Gascoigne's Memories', five pieces written to themes (truisms) supplied by friends when the poet re-entered Gray's Inn in 1565/6. All of them have their merits; the third, on the theme *magnum vectigal parcimonia*, translated by Gascoigne as 'sparing yields a goodly rent', has been most admired. One reason is the plain, colloquial vigour of the language. What the poem does is test the epigram with its proverbial opposite, 'spend and God will send', and in getting from one to the other coins lines of wise advice which sound like proverbs themselves. It is almost as if the whole poem were an exercise in the proverbial style. If the 'truth of the truism' emerges, it

15

does so out of a considerable alertness to its formal qualities, the miniature narrative in particular:

> For he that raps a royal on his cap,
> Before he put one penny in his purse,
> Had need turn quick and broach a better tap,
> Or else his drink may chance go down the worse.

The self-conscious Englishness of the vocabulary is important too. In his informal 'Certain Notes of Instruction concerning the Making of English Verse' Gascoigne notices 'the most ancient English words are of one syllable, so that the more monosyllables that you use, the truer Englishman you shall seem, and the less you shall smell of the inkhorn'. This echoes a thought in the epistle 'To the Reverend Divines', also published as part of *The Posies*: 'although I be sometimes constrained for the cadence of rhymes, or *per licentiam Poeticam*, to use an inkhorn term, or a strange word: yet hope I that it shall be apparent I have rather regard to make our native language commendable in itself, than gay with the feathers of strange birds'. This ambition is part of what we have become familiar with since R. F. Jones's *The Triumph of the English Language*: the growing sense among English poets and thinkers that English is broad and eloquent enough for all kinds of discourse, without needing special injections of Latinate vocabulary and diction to boost its muscle power. Historically, it is also linked to a rise in English patriotism and national self-consciousness, whether grandly mythological, like the entertainment for the Queen at Kenilworth, for which Gascoigne was an actor and scriptwriter; or bluffly chauvinistic, like the remarks about the Dutch in the war poems. It is the straightforwardness that really appeals to him. A native Englishness is one guarantee of honesty.

All plain style writing needs an implied opposite, say a rhetorical grandeur which runs the risk of hypocrisy or flattery or over-inflation. The plain style is the opposite of these excesses; or the expression of some powerful emotion which is the more powerful because of the effect of its being restrained by understatement. At its worst it is banal, insensitive, naively moralistic. Gascoigne gives us the whole range.

One could agree with Winters, that the Petrarchan tradition is not the most admirable or central in sixteenth-century

16

poetry, and yet still feel that the plain, aphoristic lyric will not account for all the best short poems in the English Renaissance. It is true that there is a tendency for modern critical methods to prefer the complex and multivalent above the plain (New Critical and deconstructionist alike), but even from the period itself we can see some justice in Gabriel Harvey's comment, a marginal note to *Certain Notes*: 'A great grace and majesty in longer words, so they be current English. Monosyllables are good to make up a hobbling and huddling verse.' And he adds, with characteristic self-confidence, that Sidney and Spenser agree with him. Spenser is an interesting comparative case. Chaucer remains an important reference point for him, as he was for Wyatt and Gascoigne; and so were the fashionable Italians, Ariosto and Petrarch. (Chaucer, we sometimes forget, was a contemporary of Petrarch.) Spenser's language in *The Faerie Queene* has a willed, archaic quality about it; he is using older forms like epic similes as part of his deliberately singular style for the Matter of Britain. Gascoigne's archaism, in so far as one can be precise about such a term at such a fluid moment in the history of English, seems to come more naturally. This is partly because he is appealing to the colloquial, and thus something old-fashioned rather than in need of resurrection; and partly because his tendency to reach for alliteration, even within regularly stressed and rhymed iambic pentameters, comes out strongly in those poems which he seems to have composed very quickly. Those who boast of their facility, or let their friends do it for them, are clearly going to expose their habits of composition. They are also likely to seem rough and unpolished.

Smoothness—a quality Gascoigne sometimes attains but doesn't appear to value very much—is crucial to the development of verse in the century, even if it was elbowed out for a while by the 'strong lines' of Donne and his imitators, and the deliberate harshness of the new satirists of the 1590s and 1600s. As John Thompson points out in his *Founding of English Metre* (the book contains an important discussion of Gascoigne), a poet needs a regular metrical expectation in his own head and his reader's before he can start to make any interesting variations or disruptions. The new understanding of metre is not really in print until *Tottel's Miscellany* (1557), with the poems of Surrey, and Wyatt edited to smooth his

17

perceived metrical roughness. Gascoigne was the first to make any theoretical sense of the switch from the old four-stress alliterative line to the new, stress-syllable approach as perceived by the editorial pencil of Richard Tottel, and prefigured to a limited extent by Chaucer's free version of the heroic couplet ('riding rhyme' in *Certain Notes*). Gascoigne saw how a reader's expectation of the stress demanded by the metre would lead him to over-ride the natural stress of a word, with ugly consequences. Although he confused accent and quantity (the controversy over quantitative metre was still some years ahead), his classification of syllables into accented, unaccented, and those which could go either way, shows that his attention is on accent. This is right; English makes use of accent but not quantity for phonemic distinctions, and so accent is what readers perceive. In the end, the quantitative experiments of Sidney and others were probably most useful for understanding the possibilities of varying stress patterns, something Gascoigne doesn't recognize, and which makes some of his verse monotonous and unvaried to our ears. The same may be said of caesura; Gascoigne recognized and defined the basic principles, but was not in a position to see the value of variation beyond them. This is all hindsight of course; but it is precisely in this kind of literary theory that we can discern a line of progress, something I was anxious to underplay in more general literary history. There is so much else to poetry; and Gascoigne's insistence on the importance of invention at the start of *Certain Notes* is witness to that. Poetry is an empty recital of clichés and conventions unless inventiveness is central.

So far I have been discussing Gascoigne's prose as an annex to his poetry. In *Master F. J.* the relationship is more complex. After an elaborate game of covering the tracks, the story of Master F. J. and the sisters Elinor and Frances begins as little more than a linked series of poems, with the narrative gaps filled in by prose commentary. The inventor of the short-range sonnet sequence is expanding the concept into a linked poem sequence, where, instead of eliding the narrative links, he makes them explicit. The result is that we read the poems via the history, rather than the history via the poems, as with Sidney's or Spenser's sequences. There is a further, ironic perspective offered on the poems (and here I follow

Robert P. Adams's essay), that of the comments of the narrator, G. T. After a poem of F. J.'s, apparently composed in the white heat of passion, G. T. will offer some laconic remarks about its literary skill or originality, which immediately undermine our sense of its simple transparency.

G. T. is not just critic and link man; his role in the fictional strategy of *Master F. J.* is more interesting. There is an elaborate game of letters and sources at the beginning to show how the story got to the printers, how G. T. was able to know what happened even when his friend F. J. was asleep, leading to the opening episodes, which themselves are like well-rehearsed moves in a game. F. J. ('Freeman Jones', suggests G. T., i.e., 'John Smith') visits the house of a Lord. It appears that he is intended for his host's daughter Frances, whose pert personality makes an immediate impact, though the sensual charms of her married sister Elinor stir him more deeply. Their courtship displays the old courtly love ambivalence—the language of service and devotion masking desire, and, eventually, adultery. But it doesn't last. F. J. takes to his bed like Troilus and a whole tradition of lovesick romance heroes, and we recognize that Frances has fallen in love with him too, and while he gets some comfort from Elinor, Frances would give him all the comfort he could take. In a scene reminiscent of the 'love debates' in Castiglione, she tries telling a parabolic story that will make him see the foolishness and immorality of his position. They even give each other the names of Hope and Trust, but his persisting with Elinor makes this into an ironic statement of the values of genuine love which he has rejected. In the end it is not Elinor's husband but her secretary who is the decisive rival; G. T.'s language in describing him effectively displays the physical disgust this misshapen sexual athlete arouses in him. The whole affair blows up: F. J. leaves the house, and the worthy Frances is left with little hope for the future.

In the 1575 version, Gascoigne has cleaned up some of the more obscene passages, and set the tale in Italy, with another fiction, that it is a translation from Bartello. There is an argument that this is a shift to avoid accusations that he was attacking certain prominent contemporaries in the first version; but it seems to me that it is the moral rather than the court censors that he is trying to appease, and resetting the tale in Italy was part of this strategy, as the morality of Italians was notoriously lax as far as Elizabethans were concerned, and what went on there could hardly expect to conform to English standards. He also points up the moral of the story more explicitly. Franceschina actually dies of a broken heart after F. J. leaves, and the contrast between her and her lascivious and deceptive sister is more complete.

There doesn't seem much point in labelling *Master F.J.* the first English novel, unless the previous speaker has cited *Euphues*, which is later and less entertaining. (Though it must be noticed that Gascoigne writes the occasional 'euphuistic' sentence.) Formally, it caused no stir. People knew how to read it, as Harvey's annotations demonstrate. Many of its elements can be found in prose narratives of the period, whether translated or original. *F. J.* differs from them in quality, both of the interpolated poems, and the degree of psychological interest; and, indeed, in its literary self-consciousness, a quality much prized by critics nowadays.

Gascoigne was good at telling a story. The narratives in the Dutch campaign poems, *Master F. J.*, and the *Complaint of Philomene*—all of them have a pleasing directness, a sense of pace, and a grasp of the roles a narrator might play. Gascoigne's eyewitness account of the spoil of Antwerp is in some ways the high point of that achievement. Geoffrey Parker, in his history of *The Dutch Revolt*, describes the brutal sack of November 1576 as 'one of the worst atrocities of the sixteenth century'; a considerable corpus of anti-Spanish propaganda sprang from it. Gascoigne does not spare the Spanish from his position as semi-official government observer; and yet his account doesn't display the anecdotal, chauvinist vituperativeness of his attack on them in the poem of advice to Bat Withipoll. He realizes that a plain account will do more to convey the suddenness of the attack, and the subsequent cruelty and greed of the attackers. Only at the end does he permit himself the reflection on the possibility of God's judgement, thus showing his anger—'for surely their boasting and bragging of iniquity, is over great to escape long unscourged'.

The theme of God's judgement bulks larger in Gascoigne's later work, culminating in the compilation *The Drum of Doomsday*; and, within his own original work, in *The Glass of Government*. The *Glass* is in the tradition of the 'Prodigal

Son' drama particularly popular in the Netherlands, so it may indicate that while Gascoigne was publicly slandering the Dutch for their drunken incompetence, he was quietly absorbing the humanism and Calvinism of the home of the Northern Renaissance. The plot of the *Glass* is about judgement rather than redemption. As Robert Helgerson points out in his study of *The Elizabethan Prodigals*, 'Not the parable of the Prodigal Son, with its benign vision of personal forgiveness, but rather the paradigm of prodigal rebellion interested the Elizabethans.' And so in this play; although the fathers conclude in a forgiving attitude, Gascoigne's plot structure does not. The two elder sons are, respectively, executed for robbery, and whipped and banished for fornication; the younger sons, a bit slower intellectually but full of integrity, become respectively secretary to the Palsgrave (a local ruler) and a preacher in Geneva.

Critics have remarked how this double ending prefigures the Elizabethan and Jacobean tragicomedy; but, of course, it doesn't have the moral agnosticism so common in the developed genre. The *Glass* is a Calvinist-Humanist morality play on the confluence of religion, morality and true learning.

Gascoigne's other two plays are translations. *Jocasta*, a joint effort with his Gray's Inn friend Francis Kinwelmarshe, is from an Italian version of Euripides' play. Early Elizabethan tragedy took more from Seneca than from the Greeks when it came to classical sources, with a consequent emphasis on the unstable combination of violence and a highly rhetorical moral tone. This version of *Jocasta* introduces a number of features from Seneca-influenced drama; some striking dumb-shows to precede each act, and additional moral *sententiae* (original, or derived from Latin commonplaces). The result is Senecan Euripides in the new rhetorical manner, sententious moderation fighting bombast and violence.

The *Supposes*, translated from Ariosto and also presented at Gray's Inn, is a lively comedy of mistaken intentions and identities. Here, the sententiousness has an extra satirical edge: 'Sir, he that will go to the law, must be sure of four things: first, a right and a just cause: then a righteous advocate to plead: next, favour *coram Iudice* [before the judge]: and above all, a good purse to procure it.' (IV, viii) The play's morality is somewhat more liberal than Gascoigne's later work.

21

Erostrato, in the disguise of his own servant, has enjoyed Polynesta a number of times despite his fear that the weak-sighted fifty-year-old Cleander will buy his way into her affections. Eventually Cleander discovers a long-lost son (and with him a good deal of dignity in the play's treatment of him) and it all works out happily. The use of disguise, doubles and deceit, the faithful servants, all can be seen as the seedbed of devices for the century of romantic comedy to come. It is attractively worked out here; and perhaps alone of Gascoigne's drama, might be worth reviving on the stage.

Looking at the work as a whole, though, Gascoigne's most enduring character is 'Gascoigne', not to be confused with the historical figure who may often be observed sending him up from an ironic distance. He is unusually frank in labelling his poems—'Gascoigne's gardenings', 'Gascoigne's Woodman-ship' and so on. In *The Posies* anonymity and generality take over in the service of Gascoigne the moralist who is regarding the fruit of his hot youth as so many 'Weeds' (the title of a whole section of the collection) and thus distancing himself from them. The sense that 'Gascoigne' moves through different stages, tries out different roles, is reinforced by his use of posies, little tags usually in Latin appended to the poems which define the stance, and form an identifiable sequence from ardent lover to seeker for preferment to soldier-poet. The substantial prose glosses on the poems, whether Gas-coigne's or his publisher's, make reading the collection more like the experience of attending a modern poetry reading, where the convention is that the poet reveals something of the occasion which prompted the poem. But perhaps the most attractive 'Gascoigne', especially to a generation who take Leopold Bloom and Jim Dixon as their heroes, is the 'Green Knight' or the incompetent woodman mentioned at the beginning of this introduction, the man whose lack of success has made him see things more clearly; and whose remaining blind spots are quite endearing.

Gascoigne's career as a writer was quite short—maybe ten years—and in that time he displayed a versatility and innovativeness which are not only crucial to the development of Elizabethan literature, but well worth attention in their own right. It doesn't need much in the way of strenuous ad-vocacy to argue that Gascoigne has been under-represented in

anthologies and undervalued in literary histories. It is impor-
tant to admit that he is a patchy performer, too; there are
banalities, monotonies and unattractive whines which crop
up in his writing, and this selection has not completely
excluded them. But there are a lot of his poems which will
bear re-reading more than a few times; not a 'voice', as
poetry reviews used to demand of new poets, but a whole
range of them.

A note on the selection and the text

I do not think that Gascoigne's drama lends itself to the
extraction of highlights; in other respects, this is an attempt
to show the range and quality of his writing.

In all cases, the text is taken from the first editions. I have
preferred the text of the *Flowres* to that of the *Posies*, partly
because the prose notes are fuller, partly because the order
(even though this is only a selection) seems to represent
Gascoigne's intentions before the pressures of censorship.
Those poems printed from the *Posies* are unique to that
volume.

I have modernized spelling and punctuation, except that in
the poetry I have attempted to retain the metrical values indi-
cated by the old spelling by means of ellipsis, and I have also
retained more commas than a modern printer would in view of
Gascoigne's stated interest in the caesura, which these commas
indicate. I am aware that most accidentals in sixteenth-
century texts are more likely to be printer's than author's
marks, but there is some evidence that Gascoigne saw his own
work through the printers from 1575 on.

a. Bibliography

Jerry Leath Mills, 'Recent Studies in Gascoigne', *English Literary Renaissance* (1973), 322-7.

b. Editions

The Complete Works of George Gascoigne, ed. John W. Cunliffe, 2 vols., Cambridge, 1907-1910.
A Hundreth Sundrie Flowres, ed. C. T. Prouty, University of Missouri Studies, Vol. 17, 1941.
The Steele Glas and The Complainte of Philomene, ed. William L. Wallace, Salzburg Studies in English Literature, Elizabethan & Renaissance Studies 24, Salzburg, 1975.
Elizabethan Critical Essays, ed. G. Gregory Smith, 2 vols., Oxford, 1904 (Contains *Certain Notes* with Harvey's annotations).
Five Pre-Shakespearean Comedies, ed. F. S. Boas, Oxford, 1934 (Most easily available text of *Supposes*).
The Noble Art of Venerie (1575), reprinted as *Turberville's Book of Hunting*, Oxford, 1908.

c. Biography and criticism

C. T. Prouty, *George Gascoigne*, Columbia, 1942 (The standard biography, with examination of the works).
Ronald C. Johnson, *George Gascoigne*, New York, 1972.
Yvor Winters, *Forms of Discovery*, Chicago, 1967.
Robert P. Adams, 'Gascoigne's *Master F.J.* as original fiction', *PMLA* LXXIII (1958), 315-326.

Two gentlemen did run three courses at the ring for one kiss, to be taken of a fair gentlewoman being then present, with this condition: that the winner should have the kiss, and the loser be bound to write some verses upon the gain or loss thereof. Now it fortuned so that the winner triumphed, saying, he much lamented that in his youth he had not seen the wars. Whereupon the loser compiled these following, in discharge of the condition above rehearsed.

This vain avail which thou by Mars hast won,
Should not allure thy flitting mind to field:
Where sturdy steeds in depth of dangers run,
With guts well gnawen by claps that cannons yield.
Where faithless friends by warfare waxen ware,
And run to him that giveth best reward;
No fear of laws can cause them for to care,
But rob and reave, and steal without regard,
The father's coat, the brother's steed from stall:
The dear friend's purse shall picked be for pence,   10
The native soil, the parents left and all,
With *Tant tra Tant*, the camp is marching hence.
But when bare begg'ry bids them to beware,
And late repentance rules them to retire,
Like hiveless bees they wander here and there,
And hang on them who (earst) might dread their ire.
This cut-throat life (me seems) thou shouldst not like,
And shun the happy haven of mean estate:
High *Jove* (perdie) may send what thou dost seek,
And heap up pounds within thy quiet gate.   20
Nor yet I would that thou shouldst spend thy days
In idleness to tear a golden time:
Like country louts, which count none other praise,
But grease a sheep, and learn to serve the swine.
In vain were then the gifts which nature lent,
If *Pan* so press to pass Dame *Pallas'* lore:
But my good friend, let thus thy youth be spent,
Serve God thy Lord, and praise him evermore.
Search out the skill which learned books do teach,
And serve in field when shadows make thee sure: 30

Hold with the head, and row not past thy reach,
But plead for peace which plenty may procure.
And (for my life) if thou canst run this race,
Thy bags of coin will multiply apace.

Si fortunatus infoelix

*   *   *

He wrote (at his friend's request) in praise of a gentlewoman,
whose name was Phillip, as followeth.

Of all the birds that I do know,
Phillip my sparrow hath no peer:
For sit she high or sit she low,
Be she far off or be she near,
There is no bird so fair, so fine,
Nor yet so fresh as this of mine.

Come in a morning merrily
When Phillip hath been lately fed,
Or in an evening soberly,
When Phillip list to go to bed: 10
It is a heaven to hear my Phip,
How she can chirp with cherry lip.

She never wanders far abroad,
But is on hand when I do call:
If I command she lays on load,
With lips, with teeth, with tongue and all.
She chants, she chirps, she makes such cheer,
That I believe she hath no peer.

And yet besides all this good sport,
My Phillip can both sing and dance: 20
With new-found toys of sundry sort,
My Phillip can both prick and prance:
And if you say but fend cut Phip,
Lord how the peat will turn and skip.

Her feathers are so fresh of hue,
And so well pruned every day:

26

She lacks none oil, I warrant you,
To trim her tail both trick and gay.
And though her tongue be somewhat wide,
Her tongue is sweet and short beside,   30

And for the rest I dare compare.
She is both tender, sweet and soft:
She never lacketh dainty fare,
But is well fed and feedeth oft:
For if my Phip have lust to eat,
I warrant you Phip lacks no meat.

And then if that her meat be good,
And such as like do love alway:
She will lay lips thereon by-the-rood,
And see that none be cast away: 40
For when she once hath felt a fit,
Phillip will cry still, yit, yit, yit.

And to tell truth he were to blame,
Which had so fine a bird as she,
To make him all this goodly game,
Without suspect of jealousy:
He were a churl and knew no good
Would see her faint for lack of food.

Wherefore I sing and ever shall,
To praise as I have often proved,   50
There is no bird amongst them all,
So worthy for to be belov'd.
Let others praise what bird they will,
Sweet Phillip shall be my bird still.

Si fortunatus infoelix

*   *   *

The lover being disdainfully abjected by a dame of high
calling, who had chosen (in his place) a playfellow of baser
condition: doth therefore determine to step aside, and before
his departure giveth her this farewell verse.

27

Thy birth, thy beauty, nor thy brave attire,
(Disdainful dame, which doest me double wrong)
Thy high estate, which sets thy heart on fire,
Or new-found choice, which cannot serve thee long,
Shall make me dread, with pen for to rehearse,
Thy skittish deeds, in this my parting verse.

For why thou knowest, and I myself can tell,
By many vows, how thou to me wert bound:
And how for joy, thy heart did seem to swell,
And in delight, how thy desires were drowned,   10
When of thy will, the walls I did assail,
Wherein fond fancy, fought for mine avail.

And though my mind, have small delight to vaunt,
Yet must I vow, my heart to thee was true:
My hand was always able for to daunt,
Thy slanderous foes, and keep their tongues in mew.
My head (though dull) was yet of such device,
As might have kept thy name always in price.

And for the rest my body was not brave,
But able yet, of substance to allay,   20
The raging lust, wherein thy limbs did rave,
And quench the coals, which kindled thee to play.
Such one I was, and such always will be,
For worthy dames, but then I mean not thee.

For thou hast caught a proper paragon,
A thief, a coward, and a peacock fool:
An ass, a milksop, and a minion,
Which hath none oil, thy furious flames to cool,
Such one he is, a fere for thee most fit,
A wandering jest, to please thy wavering wit.   30

A thief I count him, for he robs us both,
Thee of thy name, and me of my delight:
A coward is he noted where he goeth,
Since every child is matched to him in might.
And for his pride no more, but mark his plumes,
The which to prink, he days and nights consumes.

The rest thyself, in secret sort can judge,
He rides me not, thou knowest his saddle best:
And though these tricks of mine, might make me grudge
And kindle wrath, in my revenging breast: 40
Yet of myself, and not to please thy mind,
I stand content, my rage in rule to bind.

And far from thee now must I take my flight,
Where tongues may tell, (and I not see) thy fall:
Where I may drink these dregs of thine despite,
To purge my melancholic mind withal.
In secret so, my stomach will I starve,
Wishing thee better than thou dost deserve.

                                  Spraeta tamen vivunt.

        *   *   *

The constancy of a lover hath thus sometimes been briefly
declared.

That self same tongue which first did thee entreat
To link thy liking with my lucky love:
That trusty tongue must now these words repeat,
I love thee still, my fancy cannot move.
That dreadless heart which durst attempt the thought
To win thy will with mine for to consent,
Maintains that vow which love in me first wrought,
I love thee still and never shall repent.
That happy hand which hardily did touch
Thy tender body, to my deep delight: 10
Shall serve with sword to prove my passion such
As loves thee still, much more than it can write.
Thus love I still with tongue, hand, heart and all,
And when I change, let vengeance on me fall.

                                   Ferenda Natura.

        *   *   *

Either a needless or a bootless comparison between two
letters.

Of all the letters in the Christ's cross row,
I fear (my sweet) thou lovest *B.* the best,
And though there be good letters many more,
As *A. O. G. N. C. S.* and the rest,
Yet such a liking bearest thou to *B.*
That few or none thou thinkest it like to be.

And much I muse what madness should thee move,
To set the cart before the comely horse:
Must *A.* give place, to *B.* for his behove?
Are letters now so changed from their course?   10
Then must I learn (though much unto my pain)
To read (anew) my Christ cross row again.

When first I learned, *A.* was in high degree,
A captain letter, and a vowel too:
Such one as was always a help to *B.*,
And lent him sound and taught him what to do.
For take away the vowels from their place,
And how can then the consonants have grace?

Yet if thou like a consonant so well,
Why should not *G.* seem better far than *B.*?   20
G. spelleth God, that high in heaven doth dwell,
So spell we gold and all good things with *G.*
B. serves to spell bald, bawdy, brainsick, bold,
Black, brown, and bad, yea worse than may be told.

In song, the *G.* clef keeps the highest place,
Where *B.* sounds always (or too sharp or) flat:
In *G.* sol, re, ut: trebles have trim grace,
B. serves the bass and is content with that.
Believe me (sweet) *G.* giveth sound full sweet,
When *B.* cries buzz, as is for basses meet.   30

But now percase thou wilt one *G.* permit,
As with that *G.* thou meanest *B.* to join:
Alas, alas, methinks it were not fit,
(To cloak thy fault) such fine excuse to coin.
Take double *G.* for thy most loving letter,
And cast off *B.* for it deserves no better.

Thus have I played a little with thy *B*.
Whereof the brand is mine, and mine the blame:
The wight which wounds thy wandering will is he,
And I the man that seek to salve thy name: 40
The which to think, doth make me sigh sometime,
Though thus I strive to jest it out of rhyme.

Meritum petere, grave.

*   *   *

A Riddle

A lady once did ask of me,
This pretty thing in privity:
Good sir (quod she) fain would I crave,
One thing which you yourself not have:
Nor never had yet in times past,
Nor never shall while life doth last.
And if you seek to find it out,
You lose your labour out of doubt:
Yet if you love me as you say,
Then give it me, for sure you may.

Meritum petere, grave.

*   *   *

Gascoigne's Arraignment

At Beauty's bar as I did stand,
When false Suspect accused me,
George (quod the judge) hold up thy hand,
Thou art arraigned of flattery:
Tell therefore how thou wilt be tried?
Whose judgement here wilt thou abide?

My lord (quod I) this lady here,
Whom I esteem above the rest,
Doth know my guilt if any were:
Wherefore her doom shall please me best,   10
Let her be judge and juror both,
To try me guiltless by mine oath.

Quod Beauty, no, it sitteth not
A Prince herself to judge the cause:
Here is our Justice well you wote,
Appointed to discuss our laws:
If you will guiltless seem to go,
God and your country quit you so.

Then Craft the cryer called a quest,
Of whom was Falsehood foremost fere,
A pack of pickthanks were the rest,
Which came false witness for to bear,
The jury such, the judge unjust,
Sentence was said I should be trussed.

Jealous the jailor bound me fast,
To hear the verdict of the bill,
George (quod the judge) now thou art cast,
Thou must go hence to Heavy Hill,
And there be hanged all but the head,
God rest thy soul when thou art dead.

Down fell I then upon my knee,
All flat before Dame Beauty's face,
And cried, good Lady pardon me,
Which here appeal unto your grace,
You know if I have been untrue,
It was in too much praising you.

And though this judge does make such haste,
To shed with shame my guiltless blood;
Yet let you pity first be placed;
To save the man that meant you good,
So shall you show yourself a Queen,
And I may be your servant seen.

(Quod Beauty) well: because I guess
What thou dost mean henceforth to be,
Although thy faults deserve no less
Than Justice here hath judged thee,
Wilt thou be bound to stint all strife,
And be true prisoner all thy life?

32

Yea madam (quod I) that I shall,
Lo faith and truth my sureties:
Why then (quod she) come when I call,
I ask no better warranties.
Thus am I Beauty's bounden thrall,
At her command when she doth call.

50

Ever or Never.

*   *   *

Gascoigne's Lullaby

Sing lullaby, as women do,
Wherewith they bring their babes to rest,
And lullaby can I sing too
As womanly as can the best.
With lullaby they still the child,
And if I be not much beguiled,
Full many wanton babes have I
Which must be stilled with lullaby.

First lullaby my youthful years,
It is now time to go to bed,
For crooked age and hoary hairs,
Have won the haven within my head:
With Lullaby then youth be still,
With lullaby content thy will,
Since courage quails, and comes behind,
Go sleep, and so beguile thy mind.

10

Next lullaby my gazing eyes,
Which wonted were to glance apace:
For every glass may now suffice,
To show the furrows in my face:
With lullaby then wink a while,
With lullaby your looks beguile:
Let no fair face, nor beauty bright
Entice you eft with vain delight.

20

And lullaby my wanton will,
Let reason's rule now reign thy thought,

33

Since all too late I find by skill,
How dear I have thy fancies bought:
With lullaby now take thine ease,
With lullaby thy doubts appease: 30
For trust to this, if thou be still,
My body shall obey thy will.

Eke lullaby my loving boy,
My little Robin take thy rest,
Since age is cold, and nothing coy,
Keep close thy coin, for so is best:
With lullaby be thou content,
With lullaby thy lusts relent,
Let others pay which have more pence,
Thou art too poor for such expense.   40

Then lullaby my youth, mine eyes,
My will, my ware, and all that was,
I can no more delays devise,
But welcome pain, let pleasure pass:
With lullaby now take your leave,
With lullaby your dreams deceive,
And when you rise with waking eye,
Remember Gascoigne's Lullaby.

Ever or Never.

*   *   *

I have heard Master Gascoigne's memory commended by
these verses following, the which were written upon this
occasion. He had (in the midst of his youth) determined to
abandon all vain delights and to return unto Grays Inn, thus
to undertake again the study of the common laws. And being
required by five sundry gentlemen to write in verse somewhat
worthy to be remembered, before he entered into their
fellowship, he compiled these five sundry sorts of metre upon
five sundry themes which they delivered unto him, and the
first was at request of Francis Kinwelmarsh, who delivered to
him this theme, *Audaces fortuna iuvat*. And thereupon he
wrote this sonnet following.

If yielding fear, or cankered villainy,
In *Caesar's* haughty heart had ta'en the charge,
The walls of *Rome* had not been reared so high,
Nor yet the mighty empire left so large.
If *Menelaus* could have ruled his will
With foul reproach to lose his fair delight,
Then had the stately towers of Troy stood still,
And *Greeks* with grudge had drunk their own despite.
If dread of drenching waves or fear of fire,
Had stayed the wandering prince amid his race,   10
Ascanius then, the fruit of his desire
In *Lavine* land had not possessed place,
But true it is, where lots do light by chance,
There Fortune helps the boldest to advance.

                                                        Sic tuli.

          *   *   *

The next was at request of Antony Kinwelmarsh, who delivered him this theme *Satis sufficit*, and thereupon he wrote as followeth.

The vain excess of flattering Fortune's gifts,
Envenometh the mind with vanity,
And beats the restless brain with endless drifts
To stay the staff of worldly dignity:
The beggar stands in like extremity.
Wherefore to lack the most, and leave the least,
I count enough as good as any feast.

By too too much Dan Croesus caught his death,
And bought with blood the price of glittering gold,
By too too little many one lacks breath   10
And starves in streets a mirror to behold:
So pride for heat, and povert pines for cold.
Wherefore to lack the most, and leave the least,
I count enough as good as any feast.

Store makes no sore, lo this seems contrary,
And more the merrier is a proverb eke,
But store of sores may make a malady,

And one too many maketh some to seek,
When two be met that banquet with a leek:
Wherefore to lack the most, and leave the least   20
I count enough as good as any feast.

The rich man surfeiteth by gluttony,
Which feedeth still, and never stands content,
The poor again he pines for penury,
Which lives with lack, when all and more is spent:
So too much and too little both be shent.
Wherefore to lack the most, and leave the least,
I count enough as good as any feast.

The conqueror with uncontented sway,
·Doth raise up rebels by his avarice,   30
The recreant doth yield himself a prey,
To foreign spoil by sloth and cowardice:
So too much and too little, both be vice.
Wherefore to lack the most, and leave the least,
I count enough as good as any feast.

If so thy wife be too too fair of face,
It draws one guest (too many) to thine inn:
If she be foul, and foiled with disgrace,
In other pillows prick'st thou many a pin:
So foul prove fools, and fairer fall to sin.   40
Wherefore to lack the most, and leave the least,
I count enough as good as any feast.

And of enough, enough, and now no more,
Because my brains no better can devise,
When things be bad, a small sum maketh store,
So of such verse a few may soon suffice:
Yet still to this my weary pen replies,
That I said last, and though you like it least,
I count enough as good as any feast.

Sic tuli.

*   *   *

36

John Vaughan delivered him this theme, *Magnum vectigal parcimonia*, whereupon he wrote thus.

The common speech is, spend and God will send,
But what sends he? a bottle and a bag,
A staff, a wallet and a woeful end,
For such as list in bravery so to brag.
Then if thou covet coin enough to spend,
Learn first to spare thy budget at the brink,
So shall the bottom be the faster bound:
But he that list with lavish hand to link,
(In like expense) a penny with a pound,
May chance at last to sit aside and shrink   10
His harebrained head without Dame Dainty's door.
Hick, Hob and Dick with clouts upon their knee,
Have many times more goonhole groats in store,
And change of crowns more quick at call than he,
Which let their lease and took their rent before.
For he that raps a royal on his cap,
Before he put one penny in his purse,
Had need turn quick and broach a better tap,
Or else his drink may chance go down the worse.
I not deny but some men have good hap,   20
To climb aloft by scales of courtly grace,
And win the world with liberality:
Yet he that yerks old angels out apace,
And hath no new to purchase dignity,
When orders fall, may chance to lack his grace.
For haggard hawks mislike an empty hand:
So stiffly some stick to the mercer's stall,
Till suits of silk have sweat out all their land.
So oft thy neighbours banquet in thy hall,
Till Davie Debit in thy parlour stand,   30
And bids thee welcome to thine own decay.
I like a lion's looks not worth a leek
When every fox beguiles him of his prey:
What sauce but sorrow serveth him a week,
Which all his cates consumeth in one day?
First use thy stomach to a stound of ale,
Before thy malmsey come in merchants' books,
And rather wear (for shift) thy shirt of mail,

37

Than tear thy silken sleeves with tenterhooks.
Put feathers in thy pillows great and small, 40
Let them be prinked with plumes that gape for plums,
Heap up thy gold and silver safe in hooches,
Catch, snatch, and scratch for scrapings and for crumbs,
Before thou deck thy hat (on high) with brooches.
Let first thine one hand hold fast all that comes,
Before that other learn his letting fly:
Remember still that soft fire makes sweet malt,
No haste but good (who means to multiply):
Bought wit is dear, and dressed with sour salt,
Repentance comes too late, and then say I, 50
Who spares the first and keeps the last unspent,
Shall find that sparing yields a goodly rent.

Sic tuli.

    *   *   *

Alexander Nevile delivered him this theme, *Sat cito, si sat bene*,
whereupon he compiled these seven sonnets in sequence, there-
in bewraying his own *Nimis cito*: and therewith his *Vix bene*,
as followeth.

In haste post haste, when first my wandering mind,
Beheld the glistering Court with gazing eye,
Such deep delights I seemed therein to find,
As might beguile a graver guest than I.
The stately pomp of Princes and their peers,
Did seem to swim in floods of beaten gold,
The wanton world of young delightful years,
Was not unlike a heaven for to behold,
Wherein did swarm (for every saint) a Dame,
So fair of hue, so fresh of their attire, 10
As might expel Dame *Cynthia* for fame,
Or conquer *Cupid* with his own desire.
These and such like were baits that blazed still
Before mine eye to feed my greedy will.

2
Before mine eye to feed my greedy will,
Gan muster eke mine old acquainted mates,

Who helped the dish (of vain delight) to fill
My empty mouth with dainty delicates:
And foolish boldness took the whip in hand,
To lash my life into this trustless trace,   20
Till all in haste I leapt aloof from land,
And hoist up sail to catch a courtly grace:
Each lingering day did seem a world of woe,
Till in that hapless haven my head was brought:
Waves of wanhope so tossed me to and fro,
In deep despair to drown my dreadful thought:
Each hour a day, each day a year did seem,
And every year a world my will did deem.

3
And every year a world my will did deem,
Till lo, at last, to Court now am I come.   30
A seemly swain, that might the place beseem,
A gladsome guest embraced of all and some:
Not there content with common dignity,
My wandering eye in haste, (yea post post haste)
Beheld the blazing badge of bravery,
For want whereof, I thought myself disgraced:
Then peevish pride puffed up my swelling heart,
To further forth so hot an enterprise:
And comely cost began to play his part,
In praising patterns of my own device: 40
Thus all was good that might be got in haste,
To prink me up, and make me higher placed.

4
To prink me up and make me higher placed,
All came too late that tarried any time,
Piles of provision pleased not my taste,
They made my heels too heavy for to climb:
Me thought it best that boughs of boisterous oak
Should first be shred to make my feathers gay,
Till at the last a deadly dinting stroke,
Brought down the bulk with edgetools of decay: 50
Of every far, I then let fly a lease,
To feed the purse that paid for peevishness,
Till rent and all were fallen in such disease,

As scarce could serve to maintain cleanliness:
The bough, the body, fine, farm, lease and land,
All were too little for the merchant's hand.

5

All were too little for the merchant's hand,
And yet my bravery bigger than his book:
But when this hot account was coldly scanned,
I thought high time about me for to look: 60
With heavy cheer I cast my head aback,
To see the fountain of my furious race,
Compared my loss, my living, and my lack,
In equal balance with my jolly grace,
And saw expenses grating on the ground
Like lumps of lead to press my purse full oft,
When light reward and recompense were found,
Fleeting like feathers in the wind aloft:
These thus compared, I left the court at large,
For why? the gains doth seldom quit the charge.   70

6

For why? the gains doth seldom quit the charge,
And so say I, by proof too dearly bought,
My haste made waste, my brave and brainsick barge,
Did float too fast, to catch a thing of nought;
With leisure, measure, mean, and many more,
I might have kept a chair of quiet state,
But hasty heads cannot be settled so,
Till crooked Fortune give a crabbed mate;
As busy brains must beat on tickle toys,
As rash invention breeds a raw device,   80
So sudden falls do hinder hasty joys,
And as swift baits do fleetest fish entice,
So haste makes waste, and therefore now I say,
No haste but good, where wisdom makes the way.

7

No haste but good, where wisdom makes the way
For proof whereof we see the silly snail,
Who sees the soldier's carcass cast away,
With hot assault the castle to assail,

40

By line and leisure climbs the lofty wall,
And wins the turret's top more cunningly, 90
Than doughty Dick, who lost his life and all,
With hoisting up his head too hastily:
The swiftest bitch brings forth the blindest whelps,
The hottest fevers coldest cramps ensue,
The nakedest need hath ever latest helps:
With *Nevile* then I find this proverb true,
That *haste makes waste*, and therefore still I say,
No haste but good, where wisdom makes the way.

Sic tuli.

*   *   *

Richard Courtop (the last of the five) gave him this theme,
Durum aeneum & miserabile aevum, and thereupon he wrote
in this wise.

When peerless Princes' courts were free from flattery,
The Justice from unequal doom, the quest from perjury,
The pillars of the state, from proud presumption,
The clerks from heresy, the commons from rebellion;
Then right rewards were given, by sway of due desert,
Then Virtue's dealings might be placed aloft to play their part:
Then might they count it true, that hath been said of old,
The children of those happy days were born in beds of gold,
And swaddled in the same: the nurse that gave them suck,
Was wife of Liberality, and lemman to Good Luck. 10
When *Caesar* won the field, his captains caught the towns,
And every painful soldier's purse was crammed full of crowns.
Lycurgus for good laws, lost his own liberty,
And thought it better to prefer common commodity.
But now the times are turned, it is not as it was,
The gold is gone, the silver sunk, and nothing left but brass.
To see a king encroach, what wonder should it seem,
When commons cannot be content, with country diadem?
The Prince may die a babe, trussed up by treachery,
Where vain ambition doth move trustless nobility. 20
Errors in pulpit preach, where faith in priesthood fails,
Promotion (not devotion) is cause why clergy fails.
Thus is the stage staked out, where all these parts be played,

And I the prologue should pronounce, but that I am afraid.
First *Caiphas* plays the priest, and *Herod* sits as king,
Pilate the judge, *Judas* the juror verdict in doth bring,
Vain tattling plays the Vice, well clad in rich array,
And poor Tom Truth is laughed to scorn, with garments
   nothing gay,
The woman Wantonness, she comes with ticing train,
Pride in her pocket plays bo peep, and Bawdry in her brain.   30
Her handmaids be Deceit, Danger, and Dalliance,
Riot and Revel follow her, they be of her alliance:
Next these comes in Sim Swash, to see what stir they keep.
Clim of the Clough then takes his heels, 'tis time for him to
   creep:
To pack the pageant up, comes Sorrow with a song,
He says these jests can get no groats, and all this gear goeth
   wrong:
First Pride without cause why, he sings the treble part,
The mean he mumbles out of tune, for lack of life and heart:
Cost lost, the counter tenor chanteth on apace,
Then all in discords stands the clef, and Beggary sings the
   bass.   40
The players lose their pains, where so few pens are stirring,
Their garments wear for lack of gains, & fret for lack of furring.
When all is done and past, was no part played but one,
For every player played the fool, till all be spent and gone.
And thus this foolish jest, I put in doggerel rhyme,
Because a crosier staff is best, for such a crooked time.
                                                     Sic tuli.

*   *   *

And thus an end of these five themes, wherein hath been
noted, that as the themes were sundry and altogether diverse,
so Master Gascoigne did accomplish them in five sundry sorts
of metre, yea and that seemeth most strange, he devised all
these admounting to the number of CCLVIII verses, riding by
the way, writing none of them until he came at the end of his
journey, the which was no longer than one day in riding, one
day in tarrying with his friend, and one day in returning to
Grays Inn: a small time for such a task, neither would I
willingly undertake the like. The metres are but rough in

42

many places, and yet are they true (*cum licentia poetica*) and I must needs confess that he hath more commonly been over curious in delectation, than of haughty style in his dilatations. And therefore let us pass to the rest of his works.

*   *   *

Gascoigne's gloss upon this text, *Dominus iis opus habet.*

My reckless race is run, green youth and pride be past,
My riper mellowed years begin to follow on as fast.
My glancing looks are gone, which wonted were to pry
In every gorgeous garish glass that glistered in mine eye.
My sight is now so dim, it can behold none such,
No mirror but the merry mean, can please my fancy much.
And in that noble glass, I take delight to view,
The fashions of that wonted world, compared by the new.
For mark who list to look, each man is for himself,   9
And beats his brain to hoard & heap this trash & worldly pelf.
Our hands are closed up, great gifts go not abroad,
Few men will lend a lock of hay, but for to gain a load.
Give Gave is a good man, what need we lash it out,
The world is wondrous fearful now, for danger bids men doubt.
And ask how chanceth this? Or what means all this meed?
Forsooth the common answer is, because *the Lord hath need*.
A noble gest by gis, I find it in my glass,
The same freehold our Saviour Christ, conveyed to his ass.
A text to try the truth, and for this time full fit,   19
For where should we our lessons learn, but out of holy writ?
First mark our only God, which ruleth all the roast,
He sets aside all pomp and pride, wherein fond worldlings
   boast.
He is not fed with calves, as in the days of old,
He cares but little for their copes, that glister all of gold.
His train is not so great, as filthy Satan's band,
A smaller herd may serve to feed, at our great master's hand.
He likes no numbered prayers, to purpose popish meed,
He asks no more than penitence, thereof *Our Lord hath need*:
Next mark the heathen's gods, and by them shall we see,
They be not now so good fellows, as they were wont to be. 30
Jove, *Mars*, and *Mercury*, Dame *Venus* and the rest,

They banquet not as they were wont, they know it were not
  best:
They shrink into the clouds, and there they serve our need,
As planets and signs moveable, by destinies decreed.
So kings and princes both, have left their halls at large,
Their privy chambers cost enough, they cut off every charge:
And when an office falls, as chance sometimes may be,
First keep it close a year or twain, then geld it by the fee.
And give it out at last, but yet with this proviso,
(A bridle for a brainsick jade) *durante bene placido*.   40
Some think these ladders low, to climb aloft with speed:
Well let them creep at leisure then, for sure *the Lord hath need*.
Dukes, earls, and barons bold, have learned like lesson now,
They break up house and come to court, they live not by the
  plough.
Percase their rooms be scant, not like their stately bower,
A field bed in a corner couched, a pallet on the floor.
But what for that? no force, they make thereof no boast,
They feed themselves with delicates, and at the prince's cost.
And as for all their men, their pages and their swains,   49
They cloak them up with chines of beef, to multiply their gains.
Themselves lie near to look, when any lease doth fall,
Such crumbs were meant to feed poor grooms, but now the
  Lords lick all.
And why? Oh sir, because, both dukes and lords have need.
I mock not, my text is true, believe it as your creed.
Our prelates and our priests, can tell this text with me,
They can hold fast their fattest farms, and let no lease go free.
They have both wife and child, which may not be forgot,
The scriptures say *the Lord hath need*, & therefore blame
  them not.
Then come a little lower, unto the country knight,   59
The squire and the gentlemen, they leave the country quite,
Their halls were all too large, their tables were too long,
The clouted shoes came in so fast, they kept too great a throng.
And at the porter's lodge, where lubbers want to feed,
The porter learns to answer now, hence hence *the Lord hath
  need*.
His guests came in too thick, their diet was too great,
Their horses eat up all the hay, which should have fed his neat:
Their teeth were far too fine, to feed on pork and souse,

44

Five flocks of sheep could scarce maintain good mutton for
   his house.
And when this count was cast, it was no biding here,   69
Unto the good town he is gone, to make his friends good cheer.
And welcome there that will, but shall I tell you now?
At his own dish he feedeth them, that is the fashion now,
Sideboards be laid aside, the table's end is gone,
His cook shall make you noble cheer, but ostler hath he none.
The chargers now be changed, wherein he wont to eat,
An old fruit dish is big enough to hold a joint of meat,
A salad or a sauce, to taste your cates withal,
Some strange device to feed men's eyes, men's stomachs now
   be small.
And when the tenants come to pay their quarter's rent,   79
They bring some fowl at Midsummer, & a dish of fish in Lent,
At Christmas a capon, at Michaelmas a goose;
And somewhat else at New Year's tide, for fear their lease fly
   loose.
Good reason by my troth, when gentlemen lack groats,
Let ploughmen pinch it out for pence, and patch their russet
   coats:
For better farmers fast, than manor houses fall,
The Lord hath need, then says the text, bring old ass, colt and
   all.
Well lowest now at last, let see the country lout,
And mark how he doth swink and sweat to bring this gear
   about:
His feastings be but few, cast whipstocks clout his shoen,
The wheaten loaf is locked up, as soon as dinner's done.   90
And where he wont to keep a lubber, two or three,
Now hath he learned to keep no more but Sim his son and he,
His wife and Maud his maid, a boy to pitch the cart,
And turn him up to Hallontide, to feel the winter's smart:
Dame Alison his wife doth know the price of meal,
Her bridecakes be not half so big as she was wont to steal:
She wears no silver hooks, she is content with worse,
Her pendants and her silver pins she putteth in her purse.
Thus learn I by my glass, that merry mean is best,   99
And he most wise that finds the mean to keep his tackling best.
Perchance some open mouth will mutter now and then,
And at the market tell his mate, our landlord's a zore man:

He racketh up our rents, and keeps the best in hand,
He makes a wondrous deal of good out of his own mesne land:
Yea let such pelters prate, saint *Needam* be your speed,
We need no text to answer them, but this, *the Lord hath need.*

                                              Ever or never.

*   *   *

Gascoigne's good morrow

You that have spent the silent night
In sleep and quiet rest,
And joy to see the cheerful light
That riseth in the east:
Now clear your voice, now cheer your heart,
Come help me now to sing:
Each willing wight come bear a part,
To praise the heavenly King.

And you whom care in prison keeps,
Or sickness doth suppress,
Or secret sorrow breaks your sleeps,   10
Or dolours do distress:
Yet bear a part in doleful wise,
Yea think it good accord,
And acceptable sacrifice,
Each sprite to praise the Lord.

The dreadful wight with darksomeness
Had overspread the light,
And sluggish sleep with drowsiness,
Had overpressed our might: 20
A glass wherein we may behold
Each storm that stays our breath,
Our bed the grave, our clothes like mould,
And sleep like dreadful death.

Yet as this deadly night did last,
But for a little space,
And heavenly day now night is past,
Doth show his pleasant face:

46

So must we hope to see God's face,
At last in heaven on high,   30
When we have changed this mortal place,
For immortality.

And of such haps and heavenly joys,
As when we hope to hold,
All earthly sights, all worldly toys,
Are tokens to behold:
The day is like the day of doom,
The sun, the Son of Man,
The skies the heavens, the earth the tomb
Wherein we rest till then.   40

The rainbow bending in the sky,
Bedecked with sundry hues,
Is like the seat of God on high,
And seems to tell thee news:
That as thereby he promised
To drown the world no more,
So by the blood which Christ hath shed,
He will our health restore.

The misty clouds that fall sometime,
And overcast the skies,   50
Are like to troubles of our time,
Which do but dim our eyes:
But as such dews are dried up quite,
When *Phoebus* shows his face,
So are such fancies put to flight,
Where God doth guide by grace.

The carrion crow, that loathsome beast,
Which cries against the rain,
Both for her hue and for the rest,
The Devil resembleth plain:
And as with guns we kill the crow,   60
For spoiling our relief,
The Devil so must we overthrow,
With gunshot of belief.

47

The little birds which sing so sweet,
Are like the angel's voice,
Which render God his praises meet,
And teach us to rejoice:
And as they more esteem that mirth,
Than dread the night's annoy,   70
So must we deem our days on earth,
But hell to heavenly joy.

Unto which joys for to attain,
God grant us all his grace,
And send us after worldly pain,
In heaven to have a place.
Where we may still enjoy that light,
Which never shall decay:
Lord for thy mercy lend us might
To see that joyful day.   80
Haud ictus sapio

           *   *   *

Gascoigne's Goodnight

When thou hast spent the lingering day in pleasure and delight,
Or after toil and weary way, dost seek to rest at night:
Unto thy pains or pleasures past, add this one labour yet,
Ere sleep close up thine eye too fast, do not thy God forget,
But search within thy secret thoughts what deeds did thee
    befall:
And if thou find amiss in aught, to God for mercy call:
Yea though thou find nothing amiss, which thou canst call to
    mind
Yet evermore remember this, there is the more behind:
And think how well soever it is, that thou hast spent the day,
It comes of God, and not of thee, so to direct thy way.   10
Thus if thou try thy daily deeds, and pleasure in this pain,
Thy life shall cleanse thy corn from weeds, & thine shall be
    the gain:
But if thy sinful sluggish eye, will venture for to wink,
Before thy wading will may try, how far thy soul may sink,

48

Beware and wake, for else thy bed, which soft and smooth is
made,
May heap more harm upon thy head, than blows of enemy's
blade.
Thus if this pain procure thine ease, in bed as thou dost lie,
Perhaps it shall not God displease, to sing thus soberly:
I see that sleep is lent me here, to ease my weary bones,
As death at last shall eke appear, to ease my grievous groans. 20
My daily sports, my paunch full fed, have caused my drowsy
eye,
As careless life in quiet led, might cause my soul to die:
The stretching arms, the yawning breath, which I to bedward
use,
Are patterns of the pangs of death, when life shall me refuse:
And of my bed in sundry part in shadows doth resemble
The sundry shapes of death, whose dart shall make my flesh
to tremble,
My bed itself is like the grave, my sheets the winding sheet,
My clothes the mould which I must have to cover me most
meet:
The hungry fleas which frisk so fresh, to worms I can compare
Which greedily shall gnaw my flesh, and leave the bones full
bare: 31
The waking cock that early crows to wear the night away,
Puts in my mind the trump that blows before the latter day.
And as I rise up lustily, when sluggish sleep is past,
So hope I to rise joyfully, to judgement at the last.
Thus will I wake, thus will I sleep, thus will I hope to rise,
Thus will I neither wail nor weep, but sing in godly wise.
My bones shall in this bed remain, my soul in God shall trust,
By whom I hope to rise again from death and earthly dust.
                                            Haud ictus sapio.

       *   *   *

Gascoigne's counsel given to Master Bartholomew Withipoll,
a little before his latter journey to Genoa, 1572.

Mine own good *Bat*, before thou hoist up sail,
To make a furrow in the foaming seas,

Content thyself to hear for thine avail,
Such harmless words, as ought thee not displease.
First in thy journey, jape not overmuch.
What? laughest thou *Bat*, because I write so plain?
Believe me now it is a friendly touch,
To use few words where friendship doth remain.
And for I find, that fault hath run too fast,
Both in thy flesh, and fancy too sometime, 10
Me thinks plain dealing biddeth me to cast
This bone at first amid my dogg'rel rhyme.
But shall I say, to give thee grave advice?
(Which in my head is (God he knows) full geazon)?
Then mark me well, and though I be not wise,
Yet in my rhyme, thou mayest perhaps find reason.
First every day, beseech thy God on knee,
So to direct thy stagg'ring steps alway,
That he which every secret thought doth see
May hold thee in, when thou wouldst go astray: 20
And that he deign to send thee safe retour,
And quick despatch of that which is thy due:
Let this my *Bat* be both thy Prime and Hour,
Wherein also commend to *Nostre Dieu*,
Thy good companion and my very friend,
To whom I should (but time would not permit)
Have taken pain some ragged rhyme to send
In trusty token, that I not forget
His courtesy: but this is debt to thee,
I promised it, and now I mean to pay: 30
What was I saying? sirra, will you see
How soon my wits were wandering astray?
I say, pray thou for thee and for thy mate,
So shipmen sing, and though the note be plain,
Yet sure the music is in heavenly state,
When friends sing so, and know not how to feign.
Then next to GOD, thy Prince have still in mind,
Thy country's honour, and the commonwealth:
And flee from them, which fled with every wind
From native soil, to foreign coasts by stealth: 40
Their trains are trustless, tending still to treason,
Their smoothed tongues are lined all with guile,
Their power slender, scarcely worth two peason,

50

Their malice much, their wits are full of wile:
Eschew them then, and when thou seest them, say,
Da, da, sir *K*, I may not come at you,
You cast a snare your country to betray,
And **wo**uld you have me trust you now for true?
Remember *Bat* the foolish blinkered boy
Which was at *Rome*, thou knowest whom I mean,   50
Remember eke the pretty beardless toy,
Whereby thou found'st a safe return to *Geane*,
Do so again: (God shield thou shouldst have need,)
But rather so, than to forswear thyself:
A loyal heart, (believe this as thy creed)
Is evermore more worth than worldly pelf.
And for one lesson, take this more of me,
There are three Ps almost in every place,
From which I counsel thee always to flee,
And take good heed of them in any case,   60
The first is poison, perilous indeed
To such as travel with a heavy purse:
And thou my *Bat* beware, for thou hast need,
Thy purse is lined with paper, which is worse:
Thy bills of credit will not they think'st thou,
Be bait to set *Italian* hands on work?
Yes by my fay, and never worse than now,
When every knave hath leisure for to lurk,
And knoweth thou comest for the shells of Christ;
Beware therefore, wherever that thou go,   70
It may fall out that thou shalt be enticed
To sup sometimes with a *Magnifico*,
And have a *fico* foisted in thy dish,
Because thou shouldest digest thy meat the better:
Beware therefore, and rather feed on fish,
Than learn to spell fine flesh with such a letter.
Some may present thee with a pound or twain
Of Spanish soap to wash thy linen white;
Beware therefore, and think it were small gain,
To save thy shirt, and cast thy skin off quite: 80
Some cunning man may teach thee for to ride,
And stuff thy saddle all with Spanish wool,
Or in thy stirrups have a toy so tied,
As both thy legs may swell thy buskins full:

51

Beware therefore, and bear a noble port,
Drink not for thirst before another taste:
Let none outlandish tailor take disport
To stuff thy doublet full of such bumbast,
As it may cast thee in unkindly sweat,
And cause thy hair per company to glide,   90
Strangers are fine in many a proper feat;
Beware therefore, the second *P* is pride,
More perilous than was the first by far,
For that infects not only blood and bones,
This poisons all, and minds of men doth mar,
It findeth nooks to creep in for the nonce:
First from the mind it makes the heart to swell,
From thence the flesh is pampered every part,
The skin is taught in dyers' shops to dwell,
The hair is curled or frizzled up by art: 100
Believe me *Bat*, our countrymen of late
Have caught such knacks abroad in foreign land,
That most men call them *Devils incarnate*,
So singular in their conceits they stand:
Now sir, if I shall see your membership
Come home disguised and clad in quaint array,
As with a picktooth biting in your lip,
Your brave *mustachios* turned the *Turkey* way,
A coptank hat made on a Flemish block,
A nightgown cloak down trailing to your toes,   110
A slender slop close couched to your dock,
A curtold slipper, and a short silk hose:
Bearing your rapier point above the hilt,
And looking big like *Marquis of all Beef*,
Then shall I count your toil and travel spilt,
Because my second *P*, with you is chief.
But forwards now, although I stayed a while,
My hindmost *P*, is worse than both these two,
For it both soul and body doth defile,
With fouler faults than both those other do.   120
Short tale to make, this is a double *P*,
(God shield my *Bat*, should bear it in his breast)
And with a dash it spelleth Papistry,
A per'lous *P*, and worse than both the rest:
Now though I find no cause for to suspect

My *Bat* in this, because he hath been tried,
Yet since the polshorn Prelates can infect
Kings, Emperors, Princes, and the world so wide.
And since their brazen heaven bears such a gloss,
As most that travel come home per *Papist*,   130
Or else much worse (which is a heavy loss)
Drowned in errors like an *Atheist*:
Therefore I thought it meet to warn my friend
Of this foul *P*, and so an end to *Ps*.
Now for my diet mark my tale to end,
And thank me then, for that is all my fees.
See thou exceed not in three double *Us*,
The first is wine, which may inflame thy blood,
The second, women, such as haunt the stews,
The third is willfulness, which doth no good.   140
These three eschew, or temper them always:
So shall my *Bat* prolong his youthful years,
And see long *George* again, with happy days,
Who if he be as faithful to his feres,
As he was *wont*, will daily pray for *Bat*,
And for *Pencoyde*: and if it fall out so,
That *James a Parry* do but make good that,
Which he hath said: and if he be (no, no)
The best companion that long *George* can find,
Then at the *Spa* I promise for to be   150
In *August* next, if God turn not my mind,
Where as I would be glad thyself to see:
Till then farewell, and thus I end my song,
Take it in gree, for else thou dost me wrong.

Haud ictus sapio.

*   *   *

Gascoigne's woodmanship written to the Lord Grey of Wilton
upon this occasion, the said Lord Grey delighting (amongst
many other good qualities) in choosing of his winter deer, and
killing the same with his bow, did furnish Master Gascoigne
with a cross bow cum pertinenciis, and vouchsafed to use his
company in the said exercise, calling him one of his wood-
men. Now Master Gascoigne shooting very often, could never
hit any deer, yea and oftentimes he let the herd pass by as

though he had not seen them. Whereat when this noble Lord took some pastime, and had often put him in remembrance of his good skill in choosing, and readiness in killing of a winter deer, he thought good thus to excuse it in verse.

My worthy Lord, I pray you wonder not
To see your woodman shoot so oft awry,
Nor that he stands amazed like a sot,
And lets the harmless deer (unhurt) go by.
Or if he strike a doe which is but carrion,
Laugh not good Lord, but favour such a fault,
Take well in worth, he would fain hit the barren,
But though his heart be good, his hap is not:
And therefore now I crave your Lordship's leave,
To tell you plain what is the cause of this: 10
First if it please your honour to perceive,
What makes your woodman shoot so oft amiss,
Believe me *L.* the case is nothing strange,
He shoots awry almost at every mark,
His eyes have been so used for to range,
That now God knows they be both dim and dark.
For proof he bears the note of folly now,
Who shot sometimes to hit Philosophy,
And ask you why? forsooth I make avow,
Because his wanton wits went all awry.   20
Next that, he shot to be a man in law,
And spent some time with learned Littleton,
Yet in the end, he proved but a daw,
For law was dark and he had quickly done.
Then could he wish Fitzherbert such a brain,
As *Tully* had, to write the law by art,
So that with pleasure, or with little pain,
He might perhaps, have caught a truant's part.
But all too late, he most misliked the thing,
Which most might help to guide his arrow straight,   30
He winked wrong, and so let slip the string,
Which cast him wide, for all his quaint conceit.
From thence he shot to catch a courtly grace,
And thought even there to wield the world at will,
But out alas he much mistook the place,
And shot awry at every rover still.

The blazing baits which draw the gazing eye,
Unfeathered there his first affection,
No wonder then although he shot awry,
Wanting the feathers of discretion.   40
Yet more than them, the marks of dignity,
He much mistook, and shot the wronger way,
Thinking the power of prodigality,
Had been best mean to purchase such a prey.
He thought the flattering face which fleareth still,
Had been full fraught with all fidelity,
And that such words as courtiers use at will,
Could not have varied from the verity.
But when his bonnet buttoned with gold,
His comely cap beguarded all with gay,   50
His bumbast hose, with linings manifold,
His knit silk stocks and all his quaint array,
Had picked his purse of all his Peter Pence,
Which might have paid for his promotion,
Then (all too late) he found that light expense,
Had quite quenched out the court's devotion.
So that since then the taste of misery,
Hath been always full bitter in his bit,
And why? forsooth because he shot awry,
Mistaking still the marks which others hit.   60
But now behold what mark the man doth find,
He shoots to be a soldier in his age,
Mistrusting all the virtues of the mind,
He trusts the power of his personage.
As though long limbs led by a lusty heart,
Might yet suffice to make him rich again,
But Flushing frays have taught him such a part,
That now he thinks the wars yield no such gain.
And sure I fear, unless your lordship deign,
To train him yet into some better trade,   70
It will be long before he hit the vein,
Whereby he may a richer man be made.
He cannot climb as other catchers can,
To lead a charge before himself be led.
He cannot spoil the simple sakeless man,
Which is content to feed him with his bread.
He cannot pinch the painful soldier's pay,

55

And shear him out his share in ragged sheets,
He cannot stop to make a greedy prey
Upon his fellows grovelling in the streets.	80
He cannot pull the spoil from such as pill,
And seem full angry at such foul offence,
Although the gain content his greedy will,
Under the cloak of contrary pretence:
And nowadays, the man that shoots not so,
May shoot amiss, even as your woodman doth:
But then you marvel why I let them go,
And never shoot, but say farewell forsooth:
Alas my Lord, while I do muse hereon,
And call to mind my youthful years mispent,	90
They give me such a bone to gnaw upon,
That all my senses are in silence pent.
My mind is rapt in contemplation,
Wherein my dazzling eyes only behold,
The black hour of my constellation,
Which framed me so luckless on the mould:
Yet therewithal I cannot but confess,
That vain presumption makes my heart to swell,
For thus I think, not all the world (I guess,)
Shoots bet than I, nay some shoots not so well.	100
In *Aristotle* somewhat did I learn,
To guide my manners all by comeliness,
And *Tully* taught me somewhat to discern,
Between sweet speech and barbarous rudeness.
Old *Parkins, Rastell*, and *Dan Bracton's* books,
Did lend me somewhat of the lawless law,
The crafty courtiers with their lawless looks,
Must needs put some experience in my maw:
Yet cannot these with many mast'ries more,
Make me shoot straight at any gainful prick,	110
Where some that never handled such a bow,
Can hit the white, or touch it near the quick,
Who can nor speak, nor write in pleasant wise,
Nor lead their life in *Aristotle's* rule,
Nor argue well on questions that arise,
Nor plead a case more than my Lord Major's mule,
Yet can they hit the marks that I do miss,
And win the mean which may the man maintain.

Now when my mind doth mumble upon this,
No wonder then although I pine for pain: 120
And whiles mine eyes behold this mirror thus,
The herd goeth by, and farewell gentle does:
So that your lordship quickly may discuss
What blinds mine eyes so oft (as I suppose).
But since my Muse can to my Lord rehearse
What makes me miss, and why I do not shoot,
Let me imagine in this worthless verse:
If right before me, at my standing's foot
There stood a doe, and I should strike her dead,
And then she prove a carrion carcase too,   130
What figure might I find within my head,
To scuse the rage which ruled me so to do?
Some might interpret with plain paraphrase,
That lack of skill or fortune led the chance,
But I must otherwise expound the case,
I say *Jehovah* did this doe advance,
And made her bold to stand before me so,
Till I had thrust mine arrow to her heart,
That by the sudden of her overthrow,
I might endeavour to amend my part,   140
And turn mine eyes that they no more behold,
Such guileful marks as seem more than they be:
And though they glister outwardly like gold,
Are inwardly like brass, as men may see:
And when I see the milk hang in her teat,
Methinks it saith, old babe now learn to suck,
Who in thy youth couldst never learn the feat
To hit the whites which live with all good luck.
Thus have I told my Lord, (God grant in season)
A tedious tale in rhyme, but little reason.   150

Haud ictus sapio.

      *   *   *

from Gascoigne's Gardenings

In that other end of his said close walks, were written these
toys in rhyme.

If any flower that here is grown,
Or any herb may ease your pain,
Take and account it as your own,
But recompense the like again:
For some and some is honest play,
And so my wife taught me to say.

If here to walk you take delight,
Why come, and welcome when you will:
If I bid you sup here this night,
Bid me another time, and still   10
Think some and some is honest play,
For so my wife taught me to say.

Thus if you sup or dine with me,
If you walk here, or sit at ease,
If you desire the thing you see,
And have the same your mind to please,
Think some and some is honest play,
And so my wife taught me to say.

Haud ictus sapio.

         *   *   *

In a chair in the same garden was written this following.

If thou sit here to view this pleasant garden place,
Think thus: at last will come a frost, & all these flowers deface.
But if thou sit at ease to rest thy weary bones,
Remember death brings final rest to all our grievous groans.
So whether for delight, or here thou sit for ease,
Think still upon the latter day, so shalt thou God best please.

Haud ictus sapio.

Upon a stone in the wall of his garden he had written the year wherein he did the cost of these devices, and therewithal this posy in Latin.

Quoniam etiam humiliatos, amoena delectant.

         *   *   *

Gascoigne's voyage into Holland, An. 1572, written to the
right honourable the Lord Grey of Wilton.

A strange conceit, a vein of new delight,
Twixt weal and woe, twixt joy and bitter grief,
Hath pricked forth my hasty pen to write
This worthless verse in hazard of reproof:
And to mine alderlievest Lord I must indict
A woeful case, a chip of sorry chance,
A type of heaven, a lively hue of hell,
A fear to fall, a hope of high advance,
A life, a death, a dreary tale to tell.
But since I know the pith of my pastaunce   10
Shall most consist in telling of a truth,
Vouchsafe my Lord (en bon gré) for to take
This trusty tale the story of my youth,
This chronicle which of my self I make,
To show my Lord what helpless hap ensueth,
When heady youth will gad without a guide,
And range untied in leas of liberty,
Or when bare need a starting hole hath spied
To peep abroad from mother Misery,
And buildeth castles in the welkin wide,   20
In hope thereby to dwell with wealth and ease.
But he the Lord (whom my good Lord doth know)
Can bind or loose, as best to him shall please,
Can save or spill, raise up or overthrow,
Can galled with grief, and yet the pain appease.
Which thing to prove if so my L. take time,
(When greater cares his head shall not possess)
To sit and read this ranging ragged rhyme,
I doubt not then but that he will confess,
What falls I found when last I leaped to climb.   30
In March it was, that cannot I forget,
In this last March upon the nineteenth day,
When from Gravesend in boat I gan to jet
To board our ship in *Queenborough* that lay,
From whence the very twentieth day we set
Our sails abroad to slice the salt sea foam,
And anchors weighed gan trust the trustless flood,
That day and night amid the waves we roam

To seek the coast of Holland where it stood.
And on the next when we were far from home,   40
And near the haven whereto we sought sail,
A ferly chance: (whereon alone to think
My hand now quakes, and all my senses fail)
Gan us befall: the *pilot* gan to shrink,
And all aghast his courage seemed to quail.
Whereat amazed, the master and his mate
Gan ask the cause of his so sudden change.
And from aloft the steward of our state,
(The sounding plumb) in haste post haste must range,
To try the depth and goodness of our gate.   50
Me thinks (even yet) I hear his heavy voice,
Fadom three, four foot more, foot less, that cried;
Me thinks I hear the fearful whispering noise,
Of such as said full softly (me beside)
God grant this journey cause us to rejoice.
When I poor soul, which close in cabin lay,
And there had retched till gall was well near burst,
With giddy head, my stumbling steps must stay,
To look abroad as boldly as I durst.
And whiles I hearken what the sailors say,   60
The sounder sings, fadom two full no more.
Aloof, aloof, then cried the master out,
The steersmate strives to send us from the shore,
And trusts the stream, whereof we erst had doubt.
Tween two extremes thus were we tossed sore,
And went to hull, until we leisure had
To talk at large, and eke to know the cause
What mood had made our pilot look so sad.
At last the Dutch with butterbitten jaws,
(For so he was a Dutch, a devil, a swad,   70
A fool, a drunkard, or a traitor tone)
Gan answer thus: *Ghy zijt te vroegh* here come,
Tis niet goet tijt: and standing all alone,
Gan preach to us, which fools were all and some
To trust him fool, in whom there skill was none.
Or what knew we if *Alba's* subtle brain
(So to prevent our enterprise by treason)
Had him suborned to tice us to this train
And so himself (per company and season)

60

For spite, for hate, or else for hope of gain.   80
This must we think that *Alba* would not spare
To give out gold for such a sinful deed:
And glistering gold can oftentimes ensnare,
More perfect wits than Holland soil doth breed.
But let that pass, and let us now compare,
Our own fond fact with this his foul offence.
We knew him not, nor where he wond that time,
Nor if he had pilot's experience,
Or Pilate's craft, to clear himself from crime.
Yea more than that (how void were we of sense)   90
We had small smack of any tale he told,
He poured out Dutch to drown us all in drink,
And we (wise men) upon his words were bold,
To run on head: but let me now bethink
The master's speech: and let me so unfold
The depth of all this foolish oversight.
The master spake even like a skilful man,
And said, 'I sail the seas both day and night,
I know the tides as well as others can,
From pole to pole I can the courses plight.   100
I know France, Spain, Greece, Denmark, Dansk and all,
Frize, Flanders, Holland, every coast I know,
But truth to tell, it seldom doth befall,
That English merchants ever bend their bow
To shoot at Brill, where now our flight should fall,
They send their shafts farder for greater gain.
So that this haven is yet,' quoth he, 'uncouth,
And God grant now that England may attain
Such gains by Brill (a gospel on that mouth)
As is desired:' thus spake the master plain.   110
'And since,' he said, 'myself knew not the sown,
How could I well a better pilot find,
Than this (which first) did say he dwelt in town,
And knew the way wherever sat the wind?'
While we thus talk, all sails are taken down,
And we to hull (as erst I said) gan wend,
Till full two hours and somewhat more were passed,
Our guide then spake in Dutch and bad us bend
All sails again: for now quod he (at last)
Die tijt is goet, dat heb ick weell bekend.   120

61

Why stay I long to end a woeful tale?
We trust his Dutch, and up the foresail goes,
We fall on knees amid the happy gale,
(Which by God's will full kind and calmly blows)
And unto him we there unfold our bale,
Wherein to think I write and weep for joy,
That pleasant song the hundred and seventh psalm,
There did we read to comfort our annoy,
Which to my soul (me thought) was sweet as balm,
Yea far more sweet than any worldly toy.   130
And when we had with prayers praised the Lord
Our *Edel Bloetts*, gan fall to eat and drink,
And for their sauce, at taking up the board
The ship so struck (as all we thought to sink)
Against the ground, then all with one accord
We fell on knees again to pray apace,
And therewithal even at the second blow,
(The number cannot from my mind outpace)
Our helm struck off, and we must fleet and flow.
Where wind and waves would guide us by their grace.   140
The wind waxed calm as I have said before,
(O mighty God so didst thou 'suage our woes)
The silly ship was soused and smitten sore,
With counter buffets, blows and double blows.
At last the keel which might endure no more,
Gan rend in twain and sucked the water in:
Then might you see pale looks and woeful cheer,
Then might you hear loud cries and deadly din:
Well noble minds in perils best appear,
And boldest hearts in bale will never blin.   150
For there were some (of whom I shall not say
That I was one) which never changed hue,
But pumped apace, and laboured every way
To save themselves, and all their lovely crew,
Which cast the best freight overboard away,
Both corn and cloth, and all that was of weight,
Which hauled and pulled at every helping cord,
Which prayed to God and made their conscience straight.
As for myself: I here protest my Lord,
My words were these: 'O God in heaven on height,   160
Behold me not as now a wicked wight,

A sack of sin, a wretch ywrapped in wrath,
Let no fault past (O Lord) offend thy sight,
But weigh my will which now those faults doth loath,
And of thy mercy pity this our plight.
Even thou good God which of thy grace didst say
That for one good, thou wouldst all *Sodom* save,
Behold us all: thy shining beams display,
Some here (I trust) thy goodness shall engrave,
To be chaste vessels unto thee alway,   170
And so to live in honour of thy name:'
Believe me Lord, thus to the Lord I said.
But there were some (alas the more their blame)
Which in the pump their only comfort laid,
And trusted that to turn our grief to game.
'Alas,' quod I, 'our pump good God must be
Our sail, our stern, our tackling, and our trust.'
Some other cried to clear the shipboat free,
To save the chief and leave the rest in dust.
Which word once spoke (a wondrous thing to see)   180
All haste post haste, was made to have it done:
And up it comes in haste much more than speed.
There did I see a woeful work begun,
Which now (even now) doth make my heart to bleed.
Some made such haste that in the boat they won,
Before it was above the hatches brought.
Strange tale to tell, what haste some men shall make
To find their death before the same be sought.
Some twixt the boat and ship their bane do take,
Both drowned and slain with brains for haste crushed out. 190
At last the boat half freighted in the air
Is hoist aloft, and on the seas down set,
When I that yet in God could not despair,
Still plied the pump, and patiently did let
All such take boat as thither made repair.
And herewithal I safely may protest
I might have won the boat as well as one,
And had that seemed a safety for the rest
I should percase even with the first have gone,
But when I saw the boat was over-pressed   200
And pestered full with more than it might bear,
And therewithal with cheerful look might see

My chief companions whom I held most dear
(Whose company had hither trained me)
Abiding still aboard our ship yfere:
'Nay then' quoth I 'good God thy will be done,
For with my feres I will both live and die.'
And ere the boat far from our sight was gone
The wave so wrought, that they which thought to flee
And so to scape, with waves were overrun.   210
Lo how he strives in vain that strives with God,
For there we lost the flower of the band,
And of our crew full twenty souls and odd,
The sea sucks up, while we on hatches stand
In smarting fear to feel that self same rod.
Well on (as yet) our battered bark did pass,
And brought the rest within a mile of land,
Then thought I sure now need not I to pass,
For I can swim and so escape this sand.
Thus did I deem all careless like an ass,   220
When suddenly the wind our foresail took,
And turned about and brought us eft to seas.
Then cried we all 'Cast out the anchor hook,
And here let bide, such help as God may please:'
Which anchor cast, we soon the same forsook,
And cut it off, for fear lest thereupon
Our ship should bouge, then called we fast for fire,
And so discharged our great guns everychone,
To warn the town thereby of our desire:
But all in vain, for succour sent they none.   230
At last a *Hoy* from sea came flinging fast
And towards us held course as straight as a line.
Then might you see our hands to heaven up cast
To render thanks unto the power divine,
That so vouchsafe to save us yet at last:
But when this *Hoy* gan (well near) board our bark,
And might perceive what peril we were in,
It turned away and left us still in carke,
This tale is true (for now to lie were sin)
It left us there in dread and dangers dark.   240
It left us so, and that within the sight
And hearing both of all the pier at *Brill*.
Now ply thee pen, and paint the foul despite

64

Of drunken Dutchmen standing there even still,
For whom we came in their cause for to fight,
For whom we came their state for to defend
For whom we came as friends to grieve their foes,
They now disdained (in this distress) to lend
One helping boat for to assuage our woes,
They saw our harms the which they would not mend,   250
And had not been that God even then did raise
Some instruments to succour us at need,
We had been sunk and swallowed all in seas.
But God's will was (in way of our good speed)
That on the pier (lamenting our misease)
Some English were, whose naked swords did force
The drunken Dutch, the cankered churls to come,
And so at last (not moved by remorse,
But forced by fear) they sent us succour some:
Some must I say: and for to tell the course,   260
They sent us succour sauced with sour despite,
They saved our lives and spoiled us of the rest,
They stale our goods by day and eke by night,
They showed the worst and closely kept the best.
And in this time (this treason must I write)
Our pilot fled, but how? not empty handed:
He fled from us, and with him did convey
A hoy full fraught (whiles we meanwhile were landed)
With powder, shot, and all our best array:
This skill he had, for all he set us sanded.   270
And now my Lord, declare your noble mind,
Was this a *pilot*, or a *Pilate* judge?
Or rather was he not of *Judas'* kind:
Who left us thus and close away could trudge?
Well, at the *Brill* to tell you what we find,
The Governor was all bedewed with drink,
His trulls and he were all laid down to sleep,
And we must shift, and of ourselves must think
What mean was best, and how we best might keep
That yet remained: the rest was close in clink.   280
Well, on our knees with trickling tears of joy,
We gave God thanks: and as we might, did learn
What might be found in every pynke and hoy.
And thus my Lord, your honour may discern

Our perils past, and how in our annoy
God saved me your Lordship's bound for ever,
Who else should not be able now to tell,
The state wherein this country doth persever,
Ne how they seem in careless minds to dwell,
(So did they earst and so they will do ever)   290
And to my Lord for to bewray my mind
Me thinks they be a race of bullbeef born,
Whose hearts their *butter* mollifieth by kind,
And so the force of beef is clean outworn:
As eke their brains with double beer are lined:
So that they march bumbast with buttered beer,
Like sops of browess puffed up with froth
Where inwardly they be but hollow gear,
As weak as wind, which with one puff up goeth.
And yet they brag and think they have no peer,   300
Because *Harlem* hath hitherto held out,
Although indeed (as they have suffered *Spain*)
The end thereof even now doth rest in doubt.
Well as for that, let it (for me) remain
In God his hands, whose hand hath brought me out,
To tell my Lord this tale now ta'en in hand,
As how they train their treason all in drink,
And when themselves for drink can scarcely stand,
Yet suck out secrets (as themselves do think)
From guests, the best (almost) in all their land,   310
(I name no man, for that were broad before)
Will (as men say) enure the same sometime,
But surely this (or I mistake him sore)
Or else he can (but let it pass in rhyme)
Dissemble deep, and mock sometimes the more.
Well, drunkenness is here good company,
And therewithal *per consequence* it falls,
That whoredom is accounted jollity:
A gentle state, where two such tennis balls
Are tossed still and better balls let lie.   320
I cannot herewith from my Lord conceal,
How *God* and *Mammon* here do dwell yfeare,
And how the *Mass* is cloaked under veil
Of policy, till all the coast be clear;
Ne can I choose, but I must ring a peal,

66

To tell what hypocrites the nuns there be:
And how the old nuns be content to go,
Before a man in streets like mother B,
Until they come whereas there dwells a *Ho*,
(*Re*: ceive that half and let the rest go free)   330
There can they point with finger as they pass,
Yea sir sometimes they can come in themself,
To strike the bargain 'tween a wanton lass,
And *Edel Bloetts*: now is not this good pelf?
As for the young nuns, they be bright as glass,
And chaste forsooth: *met v*: and *anders niet*,
What said I? What? That is a mystery,
I may no verse of such a theme indict,
Young *Roland Yorke* may tell it bet' than I,
Yet to my Lord this little will I write,   340
That though I have (myself) no skill at all,
To take the countenance of a *colonel*,
Had I a good *lieutenant general*,
As good *John Zouche* wherever that he dwell,
Or else *Ned Denny*, (fair mought him befall)
I could have brought a noble regiment,
Of smugskinned nuns into my country soil,
But farewell they as things impertinent,
Let them (for me) go dwell with Master *Moyle*
Who hath behight to place them well in Kent.   350
And I shall well my silly self content,
To come alone unto my lovely Lord,
And unto him (when rhyming sport is spent)
To tell some sad and reasonable word,
Of *Holland's* state, the which I will present,
In carts, in maps, and eke in models made,
If God of heaven my purpose not prevent.
And in mean while although my wits do wade
In ranging rhyme, and fling some folly forth,
I trust my Lord will take it yet in worth.   360

                                     Haud ictus sapio.

*   *   *

from Dan Bartholomew of Bath

from 'The Reporter'

. . . For though he had in all his learned lore
Both read good rules to bridle fantasy,
And all good authors taught him evermore,
To love the mean, and leave extremity,
Yet kind had lent him such a quality,
That at the last he quite forgat his books,
And fastened fancy with the fairest looks.

For proof, when green youth leapt out of his eye   50
And left him now a man of middle age,
His hap was yet with wand'ring looks to spy
A fair young imp of proper personage,
Eke born (as he) of honest parentage:
And truth to tell, my skill it cannot serve,
To praise her beauty as it did deserve.

First for her head, the hairs were not of gold,
But of some other metal far more fine,
Whereof each crinet seemeth to behold,
Like glittering wires against the sun that shine,   60
And therewithal the blazing of her eyne,
Was like the beams of *Titan*, truth to tell,
Which glads us all that in this world do dwell.

Upon her cheeks the lily and the rose
Did entremeet, with equal change of hue,
And in her gifts no lack can I suppose,
But that at last (alas) she was untrue.
Which flinging fault, because it is not new,
Nor seldom seen in kits of *Cressid's* kind,
I marvel not, nor bear it much in mind.   70

Dame Nature's fruits, wherewith her face was fraught,
Were so frostbitten with the cold of craft,
That all (save such as *Cupid's* snares had caught)
Might soon espy the feathers of his shaft:
But *Bartholmew* his wits had so bedaft,

That all seemed good which might of her be gotten,
Although it proved no sooner ripe than rotten.

That mouth of hers which seemed to flow with mell,
In speech, in voice, in tender touch, in taste,
That dimpled chin wherein delight did dwell   80
That ruddy lip wherein was pleasure placed,
Those well-shaped hands, fine arms and slender waist;
With all the gifts which gave her any grace
Were smiling baits which caught fond fools apace.

Why strive I then to paint her name with praise?
Since form and fruits were found so far unlike,
Since of her cage Inconstance kept the keys,
And Change had cast her honour down in dike:
Since fickle kind in her the stroke did strike,
I may no praise unto a knife bequeath,   90
With rust yfret, though painted be the sheath.

But since I must a name to her assign
Let call her now *Ferenda Natura*,
And if thereat she seem for to repine,
No force at all, for hereof I am sure a,
That since her pranks were for the most impure a,
I can appoint her well no better name,
Than this, wherein Dame *Nature* bears the blame.

And thus I say, when *Bartholmew* had spent
His pride of youth (untied in links of love)   100
Behold now happy contrary to intent,
(Or destinies ordained from above
From which no wight on earth may well remove)
Presented to his view this fiery dame,
To kindle coals where earst had been no flame.

Whom when he saw to shine in seemly grace,
And therewithal gan mark her tender youth,
He thought not like, that under such a face
She could convey the treason of untruth:
Whereby he vowed (alas the more his ruth)
Lo serve this saint for term of all his life,
Lo here both root and rind of all his strife . . .

'Dan Bartholomew's Dolorous Discourses'

I have entreated care to cut the thread
Which all too long hath held my ling'ring life,
And here aloof now have I hid my head,
From company, thereby to stint my strife.
This solitary place doth please me best,
Where I may wear my willing mind with moan,
And where the sighs which boil out of my breast,
May scald my heart, and yet the cause unknown.
All this I do, for thee my sweetest sour,
For whom (of yore) I counted not of care,   10
For whom with hungry jaws I did devour
The secret bait which lurked in the snare:
For whom I thought all foreign pleasures pain,
From whom again, all pain did pleasure seem,
But only thine, I found all fancies vain,
But only thine, I did no colours deem.
Such was the rage, that whilom did possess
The privy corners of my mazed mind:
When hot desire, did count those torments less
Which gained the gaze that did my freedom bind. 20
And now (with care) I can record those days,
And call to mind the quiet life I led
Before I first beheld thy golden rays,
When thine untruth yet troubled not my head.
Remember then, as I cannot forget,
How I had laid, both love, and lust aside,
And how I had my fired fancy set,
In constant vow, for ever to abide.
The bitter proof of pangs in pleasure past,
The costly taste, of honey mixed with gall;   30
The painted heaven, which turned to hell at last
The freedom feigned, which brought me but to thrall,
The ling'ring suit, well fed with fresh delays
The wasted vows which fled with every wind:
The restless nights, to purchase pleasing days,
The toiling days to please my restless mind.
All these (with more) had bruised so my breast,

70

And graft such grief within my groaning heart,
That I had left Dame Fancy and the rest
To greener years, which might endure the smart.   40
My weary bones did bear away the scars,
Of many a wound, received by disdain:
So that I found the fruit of all those wars,
To be naught else but pangs of unknown pain,
And now mine eyes were shut from such delight,
My fancy faint, my hot desires were cold,
When cruel hap, presented to my sight,
Thy maiden's face, in years which were not old.
I think the Goddess of Revenge devised,
So to be wreaked on my rebelling will,   50
Because I had in youthful years despised,
To taste the baits, which 'ticed my fancy still.
How so it were, God knows, I cannot tell:
But if I lie, you heavens, the plague be mine,
I saw no sooner, how delight did dwell
Between those little infant's eyes of thine,
But straight a sparkling coal of quick desire,
Did kindle flame within my frozen heart,
And yielding fancy softly blew the fire,
Which since hath been the cause of all my smart.   60
What need I say? thyself for me can swear
How much I tendered thee in tender years:
Thy life was then to me (God knows) full dear,
My life to thee is light, as now appears.
I loved thee first, and shall do to my last,
Thou flattered'st first, and so thou wouldst do still;
For love of thee full many pains I passed,
For deadly hate thou seekest me to kill.
I cannot now, with manly tongue rehearse,
How soon that melting mind of thine did yield,   70
I shame to write, in this waymenting verse,
With how small fight, I vanquished thee in field:
But *Caesar* he, which all the world subdued,
Was never yet so proud of victory,
Nor *Hannibal*, with martial fears endued,
Did so much please himself in policy,
As I (poor I) did seem to triumph then,
When first I got the bulwarks of thy breast,

With hot alarms I comforted my men,
In foremost rank I stood before the rest,   80
And shook my flag, not all to show my force,
But that thou might'st thereby perceive my mind;
Askances lo, now could I kill thy corse,
And yet my life, is unto thee resigned.
Well let them pass, and think upon the joy,
The mutual love, the confidence, the trust,
Whereby we both abandoned annoy,
And fed our minds with fruits of lovely lust.
Think on the tithe, of kisses got by stealth,
Of sweet embracings shortened by fear,   90
Remember that which did maintain our health,
Alas, alas why should I name it here?
And in the midst of all those happy days,
Do not forget the changes of my chance,
When in the depths of many wayward ways,
I only sought, what might thy state advance.
Thou must confess, how much I cared for thee,
When of myself, I cared not for myself,
And when my hap was in mishaps to be,
Esteemed thee more, than all the worldly pelf.   100
Mine absent thoughts did beat on thee alone,
When thou hadst found a fond and newfound choice:
For lack of this I sank in endless moan,
When thou in change didst tumble and rejoice.
O mighty Gods, needs must I honour you,
Needs must I judge your judgements to be just,
Because she did forsake him that was true,
And with false love, did cloak a feigned lust.
By high decrees, you ordained the change,
To light on such, as she must needs mislike,   110
A meet reward for such as seek to range,
When fancy's force, their feeble flesh doth strike.
But did I then give bridle to thy fall,
Thou headstrong thou, accuse me if thou can?
Did not I hazard love yea life and all,
To ward thy will, from that unworthy man?
And when by toil I travailed to find,
The secret causes of thy madding mood,
I found naught else but tricks of *Cressid's* kind,

72

Which plainly prove, that thou wert of her blood.   120
I found that absent *Troilus* was forgot,
When *Diomede* had got both brooch and belt,
Both glove and hand, yea heart and all God wot,
When absent *Troilus* did in sorrows swelt.
These tricks (with more) thou knowest thyself I found,
Which now are needless here for to rehearse,
Unless it were to touch a tender wound,
With corrosives my tender heart to pierce.
But as that wound is counted little worth,
Which giveth over for a loss or twain,   130
And cannot find the means to single forth,
The stricken deer which doth in herd remain:
Or as the kindly spaniel which hath sprung
The pretty partridge, for the falcon's flight,
Doth never spare but thrusts the thorns among,
To bring this bird yet once again to sight,
And thou he know by proof (yea dearly bought)
That seld or never, for his own avail,
This weary work of his in vain is wrought,
Yet spares he not but labours tooth and nail.   140
So laboured I to save thy wand'ring ship,
Which reckless then, was running on the rocks,
And though I saw thee seem to hang the lip,
And set my great good will, as light as flocks:
Yet hauled I in, the mainsheet of the mind,
And stayed thy course by anchors of advice,
I won thy will into a better wind,
To save thy ware, which was of precious price.
And when I had so harboured thy bark,
In happy haven, which safer was than Dover,   150
The *Admiral*, which knew it by the mark,
Straight challenged all, and said thou wert a rover:
Then was I forced on thy behalf to plead,
Yea so I did, the judge can say no less,
And whiles in toil, this loathsome life I lead,
Camest thou thyself the fault for to confess,
And down on knee before thy cruel foe,
Didst pardon crave, accusing me for all,
And said'st I was the cause, that thou didst so,
And that I spun the thread of all thy thrall.   160

73

Not so content, thou furthermore didst swear
That of thyself thou never meant to swerve,
For proof whereof thou didst the colours wear,
Which might bewray, what saint you meant to serve,
And that thy blood was sacrificed eke,
To manifest thy steadfast martyred mind,
Till I perforce, constrained thee for to seek,
These raging seas, adventures there to find.
Alas, alas, and out alas for me,
Who am enforced, thus, for to repeat   170
The false reports and cloaked guiles of thee,
Whereon (too oft) my restless thoughts do beat.
But thus it was, and thus God knows it is,
Which when I found by plain and perfect proof,
My musing mind then thought it not amiss,
To shrink aside, lamenting all aloof.
And so to beat my simple shiftless brain,
For some device, that may redeem thy state,
Lo here the cause, for why I take this pain,
Lo how I love the wight which me doth hate: 180
Lo thus I live, and restless rest in Bath,
Whereas I bathe not now in bliss pardie,
But boil in bale and scamble thus in scathe,
Because I think on thine inconstancy.
And wilt thou know, how here I spend my time,
And how I draw my days in dolours still?
Then stay a while: give ear unto my rhyme,
So shalt thou know the weight of all my will.
When *Titan* is constrained to forsake,
His leman's couch, and climbeth to his cart,   190
Then I begin to languish for thy sake,
And with a sign, which may bewray my smart,
I clear mine eyes whom gum of tears hath glued,
And up on foot I set my ghostlike corse,
And when the stony walls have oft renewed
My piteous plaints, with echoes of remorse,
Then do I cry and call upon thy name,
And thus I say, thou cursed and cruel both,
Behold the man, which taketh grief for gain,
And loveth them, which most his name doth loath.   200
Behold the man which ever truly meant,

74

And yet accused as author of thine ill,
Behold the man, which all his life hath spent,
To serve thy self, and aye to work thy will:
Behold the man, which only for thy love,
Did love himself, whom else he set but light:
Behold the man, whose blood (for thy behove)
Was ever pressed to shed itself outright.
And canst thou now condemn his loyalty?
And canst thou craft to flatter such a friend?   210
And canst thou see him sink in jeopardy?
And canst thou seek to bring his life to end?
Is this the right reward for such desert?
Is this the fruit of seed so timely sown?
Is this the price, appointed for his part?
Shall truth be thus for reason overthrown?
Then farewell faith, thou art no woman's fere.
And with that word I stay my tongue in time,
With rolling eyes I look about each where,
Lest any man should hear my raving rhyme.   220
And all in rage, enraged as I am,
I take my sheet, my slippers and my gown,
And in the *Bath* from whence but late I came,
I cast myself in dolours there to drown.
There all alone I can myself convey,
Into some corner where I sit unseen,
And to myself (there naked) can I say,
Behold these brawn fall'n arms which once have been
Both large and lusty, able for to fight,
Now are they weak, and wearish God he knows,   230
Unable now to daunt the foul despite
Which is presented by my cruel foes.
My thighs are thin, my body lank and lean,
It hath no bumbast now, but skin and bones:
And on my elbow as I lie and lean,
I see a trusty token for the nones.
I spy a bracelet bound about mine arm,
Which to my shadow seemeth thus to say,
Believe not me: for I was but a charm,
To make thee sleep, when others went to play,   240
And as I gaze, thus galded all with grief,
I find it fazed almost quite in sunder,

75

Then think I thus: thus wasteth my relief,
And though I fade, yet to the world no wonder.
For as this lace, by leisure learns to wear,
So must I faint, even as the candle wasteth,
These thoughts (dear sweet) within my breast I bear,
And to my long home, thus my life it hasteth.
Herewith I feel the drops of sweltering sweat,
Which trickle down my face, enforced so,   250
And in my body feel I likewise beat,
A burning heart, which tosseth to and fro.
Thus all in flames I tinderlike consume,
And were it not that wanhope lends me wind,
Soon might I fret my fancies all in fume
And like a ghost my ghost his grave might find.
But freezing hope doth blow full in my face,
And cold of cares becomes my cordial,
So that I still endure that irksome place,
Where sorrow seethes to scald my skin withal.   260
And when from thence our company me drives,
Or weary woes do make me change my seat,
Then in my bed my restless pain revives,
Until my fellows call me down to meat,
And when I rise, my corpse for to array,
I take the glass, sometimes (but not for pride,
For God he knows my mind is not so gay)
But for I would in comeliness abide:
I take the glass, wherein I seem to see,
Such withered wrinkles and so foul disgrace,   270
That little marvel seemeth it to me,
Though thou so well didst like the noble face.
The noble face was fair and fresh of hue,
My wrinkled face is old and clean outcast:
The noble face might move thee with delight,
My wrinkled face could never please thine eye:
Lo thus of crime I covet thee to quit,
And still accuse myself of *Surquedry*:   280
As one that am unworthy to enjoy,
The lasting fruit of such a love as thine,
Thus am I tickled still with every toy.
And when my fellows call me down to dine,
No change of meat provokes mine appetite,

Nor sauce can serve to taste my meats withal,
Then I devise the juice of grapes to dight,
For sugar and for cinnamon I call,
For ginger, grains, and for each other spice,
Wherewith I mire the noble wine apace,   290
My fellows praise the depth of my device,
And say it is as good as Ippocrace.
'As Ippocrace?' say I, and then I swelt,
My fainting limbs straight fall into a swoon,
Before the taste of Ippocrace is felt.
The naked name in dolours doth me drown,
For then I call unto my troubled mind,
That Ippocrace hath been thy daily drink,
That Ippocrace hath walked with every wind
In bottles that were filled to the brink.   300
With Ippocrace thou banquetest full oft,
With Ippocrace thou mad'st thyself full merry.
Such cheer hath set thy new love so aloft,
That old love now was scarcely worth a cherry.
And then again I fall into a trance,
But when my breath returns against my will,
Before my tongue can tell my woeful chance,
I hear my fellows how they whisper still.
One saith that Ippocrace is contrary,
Unto my nature and complexion,   310
Whereby they judge that all my malady,
Was long of that by alteration.
Another saith, 'No, no, this man is weak,
And for such weak, so hot things are not best,'
Then at the last I hear no liar speak,
But one which knows the cause of mine unrest,
And faith, this man is (for my life) in love,
He hath received repulse, or drunk disdain,
'Alas' cry I; and ere I can remove,
Into a swoon I soon return again.   320
Thus drive I forth, my doleful dining time,
And trouble others with my trouble still,
But when I hear, the bell hath passed prime,
Into the bath I wallow by my will,
That there my tears (unseen) might ease my grief,
For though I starve yet have I fed my fill,

In privy pangs I count my best relief.
And still I strive in weary woes to drench,
But when I plunge, then woe is at an ebb,
My glowing coals are all too quick to quench,   **330**
And I (to warm) am wrapped in the web,
Which makes me swim against the wished wave,
Lo thus (dear wench) I lead a loathsome life,
And greedily I seek the greedy grave,
To make an end of all these storms and strife.
But death is deaf, and hears not my desire,
So that my days continue yet in dole,
And in my nights, I feel the secret fire,
Which close in embers, coucheth like a coal,
And in the day hath been but raked up,   **340**
With covering ashes of my company,
Now breaks it out, and boils the careful cup,
Which in my heart, doth hang full heavily.
I melt in tears, I swelt in chilling sweat,
My swelling heart, breaks with delay of pain,
I freeze in hope, yet burn in haste of heat,
I wish for death, and yet in life remain.
And when dead sleep doth close my dazzled eyes,
Then dreadful dreams my dolours do increase,
Methinks I lie awake in woeful wise,   **350**
And see thee come, my sorrows for to cease.
Me seems thou sayest (my good) 'What meaneth this?
What ails thee thus to languish and lament?
How can it be that bathing all in bliss,
Such cause unknown disquiets thy content?
Thou doest me wrong to keep so close from me
The grudge or grief, which grippeth now thy heart,
For well thou knowest, I must thy partner be
In bale, in bliss, in sorrow, and in smart.'
Alas, alas, these things I deem in dreams,   **360**
But when mine eyes are open and awake,
I see not thee, wherewith the flowing streams,
Of brinish tears their wonted floods do make,
Thus as thou seest I spend both nights and days,
And for I find the world doth judge me once
A witless writer of these lovers lays,
I take my pen and paper for the nonce,

78

I lay aside this foolish riding rhyme,
And as my troubled head can bring to pass,
I thus bewray the torments of my time: 370
Bear with my Muse, it is not as it was.

Fato non fortuna

The introduction to the Psalm of De Profundis

The skies gan scowl, o'ercast with misty clouds,
When (as I rode alone by London way,
Cloakless, unclad) thus did I sing and say:
Behold quoth I, bright *Titan* how he shrouds
His head aback, and yields the rain his reach,
Till in his wrath, *Dan Jove* have soused the soil,
And washed me wretch which in this travail toil.
But holla (here) doth rudeness me appeach,
Since *Jove* is Lord and king of mighty power,
Which can command the sun to show his face,   10
And (when him list) to give the rain his place.
Why do I not my weary muses frame,
(Although I be well soused in this shower,)
To write some verse in honour of his name?

      *   *   *

Gascoigne's De Profundis

From depths of dole wherein my soul doth dwell,
From heavy heart which harbours in my breast,
From troubled sprite which seldom taketh rest,
From hope of heaven, from dread of darksome hell,
O gracious God, to thee I cry and yell.
My God, my Lord, my lovely Lord alone,
To thee I call, to thee I make my moan.
And thou (good God) vouchsafe in gree to take,
This woeful plaint
Wherein I faint.   10
O hear me then for thy great mercy's sake.

O bend thine ears attentively to hear,
O turn thine eyes, behold me how I wail,
O hearken Lord, give ear for mine avail,
O mark in mind the burdens that I bear:
See how I sink in sorrows everywhere.
Behold and see what dolours I endure,

Give ear and mark what plaints I put in ure.
Bend willing ear: and pity therewithal,
My wailing voice,   20
Which hath no choice,
But evermore upon thy name to call.

If thou good Lord should'st take thy rod in hand,
If thou regard what sins are daily done,
If thou take hold where we our works begun,
If thou decree in judgement for to stand,
And be extreme to see our senses scanned,
If thou take note of everything amiss,
And write in rolls how frail our nature is,
O glorious God, o King, o Prince of power,   30
What mortal wight,
May then have light,
To feel thy frown, if thou have list to lour?

But thou art good, and hast of mercy store,
Thou not delight'st to see a sinner fall,
Thou heark'nest first, before we come to call.
Thy ears are set wide open evermore,
Before we knock thou comest to the door.
Thou art more pressed to hear a sinner cry,
Than he is quick to climb to thee on high.   40
Thy mighty name be praised then alway,
Let faith and fear,
True witness bear,
How fast they stand which on thy mercy stay.

I look for thee (my lovely Lord) therefore.
For thee I wait for thee I tarry still,
Mine eyes do long to gaze on thee my fill.
For thee I watch, for thee I pry and pore.
My soul for thee attendeth evermore,
My soul doth thirst to take of thee a taste,   50
My soul desires with thee for to be placed.
And to thy word (which can no man deceive)
Mine only trust,
My love and lust
In confidence continually shall cleave.

81

Before the break or dawning of the day,
Before the light be seen in lofty skies,
Before the sun appear in pleasant wise,
Before the watch (before the watch I say)
Before the ward that waits therefore alway: 60
My soul, my sense, my secret thought, my sprite,
My will, my wish, my joy and my delight:
Unto the Lord that sits in heaven on high,
With hasty wing,
From me doth fling,
And striveth still, unto the Lord to fly.

O Israel, o household of the Lord,
O *Abraham's* brats, o brood of blessed seed,
O chosen sheep that love the Lord indeed:
O hungry hearts, feed still upon his word,   70
And put your trust in him with one accord.
For he hath mercy evermore to hand,
His fountains flow, his springs do never stand.
And plenteously he loveth to redeem,
Such sinners all,
As on him call,
And faithfully his mercies most esteem.

He will redeem our deadly drooping state,
He will bring home the sheep that go astray,
He will help them that hope in him alway: 80
He will appease our discord and debate,
He will soon save, though we repent us late,
He will be ours, if we continue his,
He will bring bale to joy and perfect bliss.
He will redeem the flock of his elect,
From all that is,
Or was amiss,
Since *Abraham's* heirs did first his laws reject.

Ever or never

*   *   *

The Green Knight's Farewell to Fancy

Fancy (quoth he) farewell, whose badge I long did bear,
And in my hat full harebrainedly, thy flowers did I wear:
Too late I find (at last), thy fruits are nothing worth,
Thy blossoms fall and fade full fast, though bravery bring them
    forth.
By thee I hoped always, in deep delights to dwell,
But since I find thy fickleness, *Fancy* (quoth he) *farewell*.

Thou mad'st me live in love, which wisdom bids me hate,
Thou bleared'st mine eyes and mad'st me think, that faith was
    mine by fate:
By thee those bitter sweets, did please my taste alway,   9
By thee I thought that love was light, and pain was but a play:
I thought that beauty's blaze, was meet to bear the bell,
And since I find myself deceived, *Fancy* (quoth he) *farewell*.

The gloss of gorgeous courts, by thee did please mine eye,
A stately sight me thought it was, to see the brave go by:
To see their feathers flaunt, to mark their strange device,
To lie along in ladies' laps, to lisp and make it nice:
To fawn and flatter both, I liked sometime well,
But since I see how vain it is, *Fancy* (quoth he) *farewell*.

When court had cast me off, I toiled at the plough   19
My fancy stood in strange conceits, to thrive I wote not how:
By mills, by making malt, by sheep and eke by swine,
By duck and drake, by pig and goose, by calves and keeping
    kine:
By feeding bullocks fat, when price at markets fell,
But since my swains eat up the gains, *Fancy* (quoth he) *fare-
well*.

In hunting of the deer, my fancy took delight,
All forests knew, my folly still, the moonshine was my light:
In frosts I felt no cold, a sunburnt hue was best,
I sweat and was in temper still, my watching seemed rest:
What dangers deep I passed, it folly were to tell,   29
And since I sigh to think thereon, *Fancy* (quoth he) *farewell*.

A fancy fed me once, to write in verse and rhyme,
To wray my grief, to crave reward, to cover still my crime:
To frame a long discourse, on stirring of a straw,
To rumble rhyme in raff and ruff, yet all not worth a haw:
To hear it said there goeth, the *man that writes so well*,
But since I see, what poets be, *Fancy* (quoth he) *farewell*.

At music's sacred sound, my fancies eft begun,
In concords, discords, notes and clefs, in tunes of unison:
In *Hierarchies* and strains, in rests, in rule and space,
In monochords and moving modes, in *Burdens* underbass: 40
In descants and in chants, I strained many a yell,
But since musicians be so mad, *Fancy* (quoth he) *farewell*.

To plant strange country fruits, to sow such seeds likewise,
To dig and delve for new found roots, where old might well
    suffice:
To proyne the water boughs, to pick the mossy trees,
(Oh how it pleased my fancy once) to kneel upon my knees,
To griff a pippin stock, when sap begins to swell:
But since the gains scarce quit the cost, *Fancy* (quoth he) *fare-
    well*.

Fancy (quoth he) *farewell*, which made me follow drums,
Where powdered bullets serves for sauce, to every dish that
    comes,   50
Where treason lurks in trust, where *Hope* all hearts beguiles,
Where mischief lieth still in wait, when fortune friendly smiles:
Where one day's prison proves, that all such heavens are hell,
And such I feel the fruits thereof, *Fancy* (quoth he) *farewell*.

If reason rule my thoughts, and God vouchsafe me grace,
Then comfort of philosophy, shall make me change my race,
And fond I shall it find, that Fancy sets to show,
For weakly stands that building still, which lacketh grace by
    low:
But since I must accept, my fortunes as they fell,
I say God send me better speed, and *Fancy now farewell*. 60

*   *   *

from *The fruits of war*, written upon this theme, *Dulce bellum inexpertis*, and it was written by piecemeal at sundry times, as the author had vacant leisure from service, being begun at Delft in Holland, and directed to the right honourable the Lord Grey of Wilton . . .

144   Soldiers behold and captains mark it well,
How hope is harbinger of all mishap,
Some hope in honour for to bear the bell,
Some hope for gain and venture many a clap,
Some hope for trust and light in treason's lap,
Hope leads the way our lodging to prepare,
Where high mishap (oft) keeps an inn of care.

145   I hoped to show such force against our foes,
That those of *Delft* might see how true I was,
I hoped indeed for to be one of those
Whom fame should follow, where my feet should pass,
I hoped for gains and found great loss alas:
I hoped to win a worthy soldier's name,
And light on luck which brought me still to blame.

146   In *Valkenburgh* (a fort but new begun)
With others more I was ordained to be,
And far beforne the work were half way done,
Our foes set forth our sorry seat to see,
They came in time, but cursed time for me,
They came before the curtain raised were,
One only foot above the trenches there.

147   What should we do, four ensigns lately pressed,
Five hundred men were all the bulk we bare,
Our enemies three thousand at the least,
And so much more they might always prepare:
But that most was, the truth for to declare,
We had no store of powder, nor of pence,
Nor meat to eat, nor mean to make defence.

148   Here some may say that we were much to blame,
Which would presume in such a place to bide,
And not foresee (how ever went the game)

Of meat and shot our soldiers to provide:
Who so do say have reason on their side,
Yet proves it still (though ours may be the blot)
That *war seems sweet to such as know it not.*

149   For had our fort been fully fortified,
Two thousand men had been but few enow,
To man it once, and had the truth been tried,
We could not see by any reason how,
The Prince could send us any succour now,
Which was constrained in towns himself to shield,
And had no power to show his force in field.

150   Herewith we had no powder packed in store,
Nor flesh, nor fish, in powd'ring tubs yput,
Nor mead, nor malt, nor mean (what would you more?)
To get such gear if once we should be shut.
And God he knows, the English soldier's gut,
Must have his fill of victuals once a day,
Or else he will but homely earn his pay.

151   To scuse ourselves, and Coronel withal,
We did foretell the Prince of all these needs,
Who promised always to be our wall,
And bad us trust as truly as our creeds,
That all God's words should be performed with deeds,
And that before our foes could come so near,
He would both send us men and merry cheer.

152   Yea *Robin Hood*, our foes came down apace,
And first they charged another fort likewise,
Alphen I mean, which was a stronger place,
And yet too weak to keep in warlike wise:
Five other bands of English **fanteries*   *footmen
Were therein set for to defend the same,
And them they charged for to begin the game.

153   This fort from ours was distant ten good miles,
I mean such miles as English measure makes,
Between us both stood *Leyden* town therewhiles,
Which every day with fair words undertakes,

86

To feed us fat and cram us up with cakes:
It made us hope it would supply our need,
For we (to it) two bulwarks were indeed.

154   But when it came unto the very pinch,
Leyden farewell, we might for *Leyden* starve,
I like him well that promiseth an inch,
And pays an ell, but what may he deserve
That flatters much and can no faith observe?
An old said saw, that fair words make fools fain,
Which proverb true we proved to our pain.

[They fight a rearguard action, but are forced to surrender
when Leyden is barred against them. The soldiers go free, but
Gascoigne has to stay in prison for four months, perhaps in
hope that he will be ransomed. He concludes . . .]

189   These fruits (I say) in wicked wars I found,
Which make me write much more than else I would,
For loss of life, or dread of deadly wound,
Shall never make me blame it though I could,
Since death doth dwell on every kind of mould:
And who in war hath caught a fatal clap,
Might chance at home to have no better hap.

190   So loss of goods shall never trouble me,
Since God which gives can take what pleaseth him,
But loss of fame or slandered so to be,
That makes my wits to break about their brim,
And frets my heart, and lames my every limb:
For noble minds their honour more esteem,
Than worldly wights, or wealth, or life, can deem.

191   And yet in wars, such grafts of grudge do grow,
Such lewdness lurks, such malice makes mischief,
Such envy boils, such falsehood fire doth blow,
That *bounty* burns, and truth is called thief,
And good deserts are brought into such brief,
That saunder snuff which swears the matter out,
Brings oftentimes the noblest names in doubt.

192   Then whether I be one of *haughty heart*,
Or *greedy mind*, or *miser* in decay,
I said and say that for mine own poor part,
I may confess that *Bellum* every way,
Is *sweet*: but how? (bear well my words away)
Forsooth, *to such as never did it try*,
This is my theme I cannot change it I . . .

                                Tam Marti quam Mercurio

from THE NOBLE ART OF VENERIE *(1575)*

The Hare, to the Hunter

Are minds of men, become so void of sense
That they can joy to hurt a harmless thing?
A silly beast, which cannot make defence?
A wretch? a worm that cannot bite, nor sting?
If that be so, I thank my Maker then,
For making me, a beast and not a man.

The lion licks the sores of wounded sheep,
He spares to prey, which yields and craveth grace:
The dead man's corpse hath made some serpents weep,
Such ruth may rise in beasts of bloody race: 10
And yet can man, (which brags above the rest)
Use wrack for ruth? Can murder like him best?

This song I sing, in moan and mournful notes,
(Which fain would blaze, the bloody mind of man)
Who not content with harts, hinds, bucks, roes, goats,
Boars, bears, and all, that hunting conquer can,
Must yet seek out, me silly harmless hare,
To hunt with hounds, and course sometimes with care.

The hart doth hurt (I must a truth confess)
He spoileth corn, and bears the hedge adown: 20
So doth the buck, and though the roe seem less,
Yet doth he harm in many a field and town:
The climbing goat doth pill both plant and vine,
The pleasant meads are routed up with swine.

But I poor beast, whose feeding is not seen,
Who break no hedge, who pill no pleasant plant:
Who stroy no fruit, who can turn up no green,
Who spoil no corn, to make the ploughman want:
Am yet pursued with hound, horse, might and main
By murdering men, until they leave me slain.   30

Sa how sayeth one, as soon as he me spies,
Another cries *Now, now*, that sees me start,
The hounds call on, with hideous noise and cries,
The spur-galled jade must gallop out his part:
The horn is blown, and many a voice full shrill,
Do whoop and cry, me wretched beast to kill.

What meanest thou man, me so for to pursue?
For first my sin is scarcely worth a plack,
My flesh is dry, and hard for to endue,
My grease (God knoweth) not great upon my back,   40
My self, and all, that is within me found,
Is neither good, great, rich, fat, sweet, nor sound.

So that thou showest thy vaunts to be but vain,
That bragg'st of wit, above all other beasts,
And yet by me, thou neither gettest gain
Nor findest food, to serve thy glutton's feasts:
Some sport perhaps: yet *grievous is the glee
Which ends in blood*, that lesson learn of me.

. . . But that my Lord, may plainly understand,
The mysteries, of all that I do mean,
I am not he whom slanderous tongues have told,
(False tongues indeed, and crafty subtle brains)
To be the man, which meant a common spoil
Of loving dames, whose ears would hear my words
Or trust the tales devised by my pen.   50
I n'am a man, as some do think I am,
(Laugh not good Lord) I am indeed a dame,
Or at the least, a right *Hermaphrodite*:
And who desires, at large to know my name,
My birth, my line, and every circumstance,
Lo read it here, *Plain dealing* was my sire,   Not ignorant
And he begat me by *Simplicity*,   simplicity
                                                       but a thought
A pair of twins at one self burden born,   free from
My sist'r and I, into the world were sent,   deceit.
My sister's name, was pleasant *Poesis*,   Satirical
And I myself had *Satyra* to name,   poetry may
                                                       rightly be
Whose hap was such, that in the prime of youth,   called the
A lusty lad, a stately man to see,   daughter
                                                       of such
Brought up in place, where pleasures did abound,   simplicity.
(I dare not say, in court for both mine ears)   65
Began to woo my sister, not for wealth,
But for her face was lovely to behold,
And therewithal, her speech was pleasant still.   Where may be
This noble name, was called *Vain Delight*,   commonly
                                                       found a
And in his train, he had a comely crew   meeter wooer
Of guileful wights: *False Semblant* was the first,   for pleasant
The second man was, *Flearing Flattery*,   poetry, than
                                                       Vain Delight?
(Brethren by like, or very near of kin)   Such men do
Then followed them, *Detraction* and *Deceit*.   many times
Sym Swash did bear a buckler for the first,   attend upon
False witness was the second seemly page,   Vain Delight.
And thus well armed, and in good equipage,
This gallant came, unto my father's court,
And wooed my sister, for she elder was,
And fairer eke, but out of doubt (at least)   80
Her pleasant speech surpassed mine so much,
That *Vain Delight*, to her addressed his suit.

Short tale to make, she gave a free consent,
And forth she goeth, to be his wedded make,   Poetry married
Enticed percase, with glow of gorgeous show,   to Vain Delight.
(Or else perhaps, persuaded by his peers,)
That constant love had harboured in his breast,
Such errors grow where such false prophets preach.
How so it were, my sister liked him well,
And forth she goeth, in court with him to dwell,   90
Where when she had some years ysojourned,
And saw the world, and marked each man's mind,
A *deep desire* her loving heart inflamed,
To see me sit with her in seemly wise,
That company might comfort her sometimes,
And sound advice might ease her weary thoughts:
And forth with speed, (even at her first request)
Doth *Vain Delight*, his hasty course direct,
To seek me out his sails are fully bent,
And wind was good, to bring me to the bower,   100
Whereas she lay, that mourned days and nights
To see herself, so matched and so deceived,
And when the wretch, (I cannot term him bet)
Had me on seas full far from friendly help,
A spark of lust, did kindle in his breast,
And bade him hark, to songs of *Satyra*.
I silly soul (which thought nobody harm)
Gan clear my throat, and strave to sing my best,
Which pleased him so, and so inflamed his heart,   Satirical poetry
That he forgot my sister Poesis,   is sometimes
                                                      ravished by
And ravished me, to please his wanton mind.   vain delight.
Not so content, when this foul fact was done,
(Yfraught with fear, lest that I should disclose   113
His incest: and, his doting dark desire)
He caused straightways, the foremost of his crew   False semblant
With his compeer, to try me with their tongues: and flattery,
                                                     can seldom
And when their guiles, could not prevail to win   beguile satiri-
My simple mind, from track of trusty truth,   cal poetry.
Nor yet deceit could blear mine eyes from fraud,
Came *Slander* then, accusing me, and said,   120
That I enticed *Delight*, to love and lust.
Thus was I caught, poor wretch that thought none ill.
And furthermore, to cloak their own offence,

They clapped me fast, in cage of *Misery*,
And there I dwelt, full many a doleful day,
Until this thief, this traitor *Vain Delight*,
Cut out my tongue, with *Razor of Restraint*,
Lest I should wray, this bloody deed of his.

The reward of
busy meddling
is misery.

And thus (my Lord) I live a weary life,
Not as I seemed, a man sometimes of might,
But womanlike, whose tears must venge her harms.
And yet, even as the mighty gods did deign
For *Philomele*, that though her tongue were cut,
Yet should she sing a pleasant note sometimes:
So have they deigned, by their divine decrees,
That with the stumps of my reproved tongue,
I may sometimes, *Reprovers'* deeds reprove,
And sing a verse, to make them see themselves.

129

Note now &
compare this
allegory to
the story of
Progne &
Philomele.

*   *   *

I see and sigh (because it makes me sad)
That peevish pride, doth all the world possess,
And every wight, will have a looking glass
To see himself, yet so he seeth him not:
Yea shall I say? a glass of common glass,
Which glistereth bright, and shows a seemly show,
Is not enough, the days are past and gone,
That berral glass, with foils of lovely brown,
Might serve to show, a seemly favoured face.
That age is dead, and vanished long ago,
Which thought that steel, both trusty was and true,
And needed not, a foil of contraries,
But showed all things, even as they were indeed.
Instead whereof, our curious year can find
The crystal glass, which glimpseth brave and bright,
And shows the thing, much better than it is,
Beguiled with foils of sundry subtle sights,
So that they seem, and covet not to be . . .

180

190

. . . When I had with no small entreaty obtained of Master F.J. and sundry other toward young gentlemen, the sundry copies of those sundry matters, then as well for the number of them was great, as also for that I found none of them, so barren, but that (in my judgement) had in it *Aliquid Salis*, and especially being considered by the very proper occasion where-upon it was written (as they themselves did always with the verse rehearse unto me the cause that then moved them to write) I did with more labour then gather them into some order, and so placed them in this register. Wherein as near as I could guess, I have set in the first places those which Master F.J. did complete. And so to begin with this his history that ensueth, it was (as he declared unto me) written upon this occasion. The said F.J. chanced once in the north parts of this realm to fall into company of a very fair gentlewoman whose name was Mistress *Elinor*, unto whom bearing a hot affection, he first adventured to write this letter following.

G.T.

Mistress I pray you understand that being altogether a stranger in these parts, my good hap hath been to behold you to my (no final) contentation, and my evil hap accompanies the same, with such imperfection of my deserts, as that I find always a ready repulse in mine own frowardness. So that con-sidering the natural climate of the country, I must say that I have found fire in frost. And yet comparing the inequality of my deserts, with the least part of your worthiness, I feel a continual frost, in my most fervent fire. Such is then the extremity of my passions, the which I could never have been content to commit to this telltale paper, were it not that I am destitute of all other help. Accept therefore I beseek you, the earnest good will of a more trusty (than worthy) servant, who being thereby encouraged, may supply the defects of his ability with ready trial of dutiful loyalty. And let this poor paper (besprent with salt tears, and blown over with scalding sighs) be saved of you as a safeguard for your sampler, or a bottom to wind your sewing silk, that when your last needleful is wrought, you may return to reading thereof and consider the care of him who is

More yours than his own,
F.J.

This letter by her received (as I have heard him say) her answer was this: she took occasion one day, at his request to dance with him, the which doing, she bashfully began to declare unto him, that she had read over the writing, which he delivered unto her, with like protestation, that (as at delivery thereof, she understood not for what cause he thrust the same into her bosom,) so now she could not perceive thereby any part of his meaning, nevertheless at last seemed to take upon her the matter, and though she disabled herself, yet gave him thanks as etc. Whereupon he brake the brawl, and walking abroad devised immediately these few verses following.

G. T.

Fair Bersabe the bright once bathing in a well,
With dew bedimmed King David's eyes that ruled Israel.
And Salomon himself, the source of sapience,
Against the force of such assaults could make but small
    defence:
To it the stoutest yield, and strongest feel like woe,
Bold Hercules and Sampson both, did prove it to be so.
What wonder seemeth then? what stars stand thick in skies,
If such a blazing star have power to dim my dazzled eyes?
    L'envoy.
To you these few suffice, your wits be quick and good,
You can conject by change of hue, what humours feed my
    blood.

F.J.

I have heard the author say, that these were the first verses that ever he wrote upon a like occasion. The which considering the matter precedent, may in my judgement be well allowed, and to judge his doings by the effects he declared unto me, that before he could put the same in legible writing, it pleased the said Mistress Elinor of her courtesy thus to deal with him. Walking in a garden among divers other gentlemen and gentlewomen, with a little frowning smile in passing by

94

him, she delivered unto him a paper, with these words. *'For that I understand not,' quoth she, 'th'intent of your letters, I pray you take them here again, and bestow them at your pleasure.'* The which done and said, she passed by without change either of pace or countenance. *F.J.* somewhat troubled with her angry look, did suddenly leave the company, and walking into the park adjoining, in great rage began to wreak his malice upon this poor paper, and the same did rend and tear in pieces. When suddenly at a glance he perceived it was not of his own handwriting, and therewithal abashed, upon better regard he perceived in one piece written (in Roman) these letters SHE: wherefore placing all the pieces thereof, as orderly as he could, he found therein written, these few lines hereafter following.

G.T.

Your sudden departure, from our pastime yesterday, did enforce me for lack of chosen company to return unto my work, wherein I did so long continue, till at last the bare bottom did draw unto my remembrance your strange request. And although I found therein no just cause to credit your coloured words, yet have I thought good hereby to requite you with like courtesy, so that at least you shall not condemn me for ungrateful. But as to the matter therein contained, if I could persuade myself, that there were in me any coals to kindle such sparks of fire, I might yet peradventure be drawn to believe that your mind were frozen with like fear. But as no smoke ariseth, where no coal is kindled, so without cause of affection the passion is easy to be cured. That is all that I understand of your dark letters. And as much as I mean to answer.

SHE

My friend F.J. hath told me divers times, that immediately upon receipt hereof, he grew in jealousy, that the same was not her own device. And therein I have no less allowed his judgement, than commended his invention of the verses, and letters before rehearsed. For as by the style this letter of hers bewrayeth that it was not penned by a woman's capacity, so the sequel of her doings may decipher, that she had more ready clerks than trusty servants in store. Well yet as the

95

perfect hound, when he hath chased the hurt deer, amid the whole herd, will never give over till he have singled it out again. Even so F.J. though somewhat abashed with this doubtful show, yet still constant in his former intention, leased not by all possible means, to bring this deer yet once again to the bows, whereby she might be the more surely stricken: and so in the end enforced to yield. Wherefore he thought not best to commit the said verses willingly into her custody, but privily lost them in her chamber, written in counterfeit. And after on the next day thought better to reply, either upon her, or upon her secretary in this wise as here followeth.

G.T.

The much that you have answered is very much, and much more than I am able to reply unto: nevertheless in mine own defence, thus much I allege: that if my sudden departure pleased not you, I cannot myself therewith be pleased, as one that seeketh not to please many, and more desirous to please you as any. The cause of mine affection, I suppose you behold daily. For (self-love avoided) every wight may judge of themselves as much as reason persuadeth: the which if it be in your good nature suppressed with bashfulness, then mighty love grant, you may once behold my wan cheeks washed in woe, that therein my salt tears may be a mirror to represent your own shadow, and that like unto Narcissus you may be constrained to kiss the cold waves, wherein your counterfeit is so lively portrayed. For if attendance of other matters failed to draw my gazing eyes in contemplation of so rare excellency, yet might these your letters both frame in me an admiration of such divine esprit, and a confusion on my dull understanding, which so rashly presumed to wander in this endless labyrinth. Such I esteem you, and thereby am become such, and even

HE F.J.

This letter finished and fair written over, his chance was to meet her alone in a gallery of the same house: where (as I have heard him declare) his manhood in this kind of combat was first tried, and therein I can compare him to a valiant Prince, who distressed with power of enemies had committed

96

the safeguard of his person to treaty of ambassade, and suddenly (surprised with a *Camnassado* in his own trenches) was enforced to yield as prisoner. Even so my friend F.J. lately overcome by the beautiful beams of this Dame *Elinor*, and having now committed his most secret intent to these late rehearsed letters, was at unawares encountered with his friendly foe, and constrained either to prepare some new defence, or else like a recreant to yield himself as already vanquished. Wherefore (as in a trance) he lifted up his dazzled eyes, and so continued in a certain kind of admiration, not unlike the astronomer, who (having after a whole night's travail, found his desired star) hath fired his hungry eyes to behold the *comet* long looked for: whereat this gracious dame (as one that could discern the sun before her chamber windows were wide open) did deign to embolden the fainting knight with these or like words.

I perceive now (quod she) how mishap doth follow me, that having chosen this walk for a simple solace, I am here disquieted by the man that meaneth my destruction: and therewithal, as half angry, began to turn her back, when as my friend F.J. now awaked, gan thus salute her.

'Mistress,' quod he, 'and I perceive now, that good hap haunts me, for being by lack of opportunity constrained to commit my welfare unto these blabbing leaves of bewraying paper (showing that in his hand) I am here accomforted with happy view of my desired joy,' and therewithal reverently kissing his hand, did softly distrain her slender arm and so stayed her departure. The first blow thus proferred and defended, they walked and talked traversing divers ways, wherein I doubt not but my friend F.J. could quit himself reasonably well. And though it stood not with duty of a friend that I should therein require to know his secrets, yet of himself he declared thus much, that after long talk she was content to accept his proferred service, but yet still disabling herself, and seeming to marvel what cause had moved him to subject his liberty so wilfully, or at least in a prison (as she termed it) so unworthy. Whereunto I need not rehearse his answer, but suppose now, that thus they departed: saving I had forgotten this, she required of him the last rehearsed letter, saying that his first was lost, and now she lacked a new bottom for her silk, the which I warrant you, he granted: and so proferring to take an humble *congé* by *bezo las manos*, she graciously gave him the *zuccado dez labros*: and so for then departed. And thereupon recounting her words, he compiled these following, which he termed *terza sequenza*, to sweet mistress SHE.

G.T.

Of thee dear Dame, three lessons would I learn,
What reason first persuades the foolish fly
(As soon as she a candle can discern)
To play with flame, till she be burned thereby?
Or what may move the mouse to bite the bait
Which strikes the trap, that stops her hungry breath?
What calls the bird, where shades of deep deceit
Are closely caught to draw her to her death?
Consider well, what is the cause of this,
And though percase thou wilt not so confess,
Yet deep desire, to gain a heavenly bliss,
May drown the mind in dole and dark distress:
Oft is it seen (whereat my heart may bleed)
Fools play so long till they be caught indeed.

And then

It is a heaven to see them hop and skip,
And seek all shifts to shake their shackles off:
It is a world, to see them hang the lip,
Who (erst) at love, were wont to scorn and scoff,
But as the mouse, once caught in crafty trap,
May bounce and beat, against the burden wall,
Till she have brought her head in such mishap,
That done to death her fainting limbs must fall:
And as the fly once singed in the flame,
Cannot command her wings to wave away:
But by the heel, she hangeth in the same
Till cruel death her hasty journey stay.
So they that seek to break the links of love
Strive with the stream, and this by pain I prove.

For when

I first beheld that heavenly hue of thine,
Thy stately stature, and thy comely grace,
I must confess these dazzled eyes of mine
Did wink for fear, when I first viewed thy face:

98

But bold desire, did open them again,
And bade me look till I had looked too long,
I pitied them that did procure my pain,
And loved the looks that wrought me all the wrong:
And as the bird once caught (but works her woe)
That strives to leave the limed wings behind:
Even so the more I strave to part thee fro,
The greater grief did grow within my mind:
Remedyless then must I yield to thee,
And crave no more, thy servant but to be.

Till then and ever. HE F.J.

When he had well sorted this sequence, he sought opportunity
to leave it where she might find it before it were lost. And
now the coals began to kindle, whereof (but ere while) she
feigned herself altogether ignorant. The flames began to break
out on every side: and she to quench them, shut up her self
in her chamber solitarily. But as the smithy gathers greater
heat by casting on of water, even so the more she absented
herself from company, the fresher was the grief which galded
her remembrance: so that at last the report was spread through
the house, that Mistress Elinor was sick. At which news F.J.
took small comfort: nevertheless *Dame Venus* with good
aspect did yet thus much further his enterprise. The dame
(whether it were by sudden change, or of wonted custom) fell
one day into a great bleeding at the nose. For which accident
the said F.J. amongst other pretty conceits, hath a present
remedy, whereby he took occasion (when they of the house
had all in vain sought many ways to stop her bleeding) to
work his feat in this wise: first he pleaded ignorance, as though
he knew not her name, and therefore demanded the same of
one other gentlewoman in the house, whose name was Mis-
tress Frances, who when she had to him declared that her
name was *Elinor*, he said these words or very like in effect:
'If I thought I should not offend Mistress *Elinor*, I would not
doubt to stop her bleeding, without either pain or difficulty.'
This gentlewoman somewhat tickled with his words, did in-
continent make relation thereof to the said Mistress *Elinor*,
who immediately (declaring that F.J. was her late received
servant) returned the said messenger unto him with especial
charge, that he should employ his devoir towards the recovery

of her health, with whom the same F.J. repaired to the chamber of his desired: and finding her set in a chair, leaning on the one side over a silver basin: after his due reverence, he laid his hand on her temples, and privily rounding her in her ear, desired her to command a hazel stick and a knife: the which being brought, he delivered unto her, saying on this wise. 'Mistress I will speak certain words in secret to myself, and do require no more: but when you hear me say openly this word *Amen* that you with this knife will make a nick upon this hazel stick: and when you have made five nicks, command me also to cease.' The Dame partly of good will to the knight, and partly to be staunched of her bleeding, commanded her maid, and required the other gentles, somewhat to stand aside, which done, he began his orisons, wherein he had not long muttered before he pronounced *Amen*, wherewith the Lady made a nick on the stick with her knife. The said F.J. continued to another *Amen*, when the Lady having made another nick felt her bleeding began to staunch: and so by the third *Amen* thoroughly staunched. F.J. then changing his prayers into private talk, said softly unto her, 'Mistress, I am glad that I am hereby enabled to do you some service,' and therewithal with a loud voice pronounced *Amen*: wherewith the good lady making a nick did secretly answer thus. 'Good servant', quod she, 'I must needs think myself right happy to have gained your service and good will, and be you sure, that although there be in me no such desert as may draw into this depth of affection, yet such as I am, I shall be always glad to show myself thankful unto you, and now, if you think yourself assured, that I shall bleed no more, do then pronounce your fifth *Amen*,' the which pronounced, she made also her fifth nick, and held up her head, calling the company unto her, and declaring unto them, that her bleeding was throughly staunched. Well, it were long to tell, what sundry opinions were pronounced upon this act, and I do dwell overlong in the discourses of this F.J., especially having taken in hand only to copy out his verses, but for the circumstance doth better declare the effect, I will return to my former tale. F.J. tarrying a while in the chamber found opportunity to lose his sequence near to his desired mistress: and after *congé* taken departed. After whose departure the lady rose out of her chair, and her maid going about to remove the same, espied,

100

and took up the writing: the which her mistress perceiving, gan suddenly conjecture that the same had in it some like matter to the verses once before left in like manner, and made semblant to mistrust that the same should be some words of conjuration: and taking it from her maid, did peruse it, and immediately said to the company, that she would not forgo the same for a great treasure. But to be plain, I think that (F.J. excepted) she was glad to be rid of all company, until she had with sufficient leisure turned over and retossed every card in this sequence. And not long after being now tickled thorough all the veins with an unknown humour, adventured of herself to commit unto a like ambassador the deciphering of that which hitherto she had kept more secret, and thereupon wrote with her own hand and heart in this wise.

G.T.

Good servant, I am out of all doubt much beholding to you, and I have great comfort by your means in the staunching of my blood, and I take great comfort to read your letters, and I have found in my chamber divers songs which I think to be of your making, and I promise you, they are excellently made, and I assure you that I will be ready to do for you any pleasure that I can, during my life: wherefore I pray you come to my chamber once in a day, till I come abroad again, and I will be glad of your company, and for because you have promised to be my HE: I will take upon me this name, your SHE.

This letter I have seen, of her own handwriting: and as therein the reader may find great difference of style, from her former letter, so may you now understand the cause. She had in the same house a friend, a servant, a secretary: what should I name him? such one as she esteemed in time past more than was cause in time present, and to make my tale good, I will (by report of my very good friend F.J.) describe him unto you. He was in height, the proportion of two *pigmies*, in breadth the thickness of two bacon hogs, of presumption a *giant*, of power a gnat, apishly witted, knavishly mannered, and crabbedly favoured, what was there in him to draw a fair lady's liking? Marry, sir, even all in all, a well lined purse, wherewith he could at every call, provide such pretty conceits as pleased her peevish fantasy, and by that means he had throughly (long before) insinuated himself with this amorous dame. This manling, this minion, this slave, this secretary, was now by occasion ridden to London forsooth: and though his absence was to her a disfurnishing of eloquence: it was yet unto F.J. an opportunity of good advantage, for when he perceived the change of her style, and thereby grew in some suspicion that the same proceeded by the absence of her chief chancellor, he thought good now to smite while the iron was hot, and to lend his mistress such a pen in her secretary's absence, as he should never be able at his return to amend the well inviting thereof, whereof according to her command he repaired once every day to her chamber, at the least, whereas he guided himself so well and could devise such store of sundry pleasures and pastimes, that he grew in favour not only with his desired, but also with the rest of the gentlewomen. And one day passing the time amongst them, their play grew to this end, that his mistress, being Queen, demanded of him these three questions. 'Servant,' quod she, 'I charge you, as well upon your allegiance being now my subject, as also upon your fidelity, having vowed your service unto me that you answer me these three questions, by the very truth of your secret thought. First, what thing in this universal world doth most rejoice and comfort you?' F.J. abasing his eyes towards the ground, took good advisement in his answer, when a fair gentlewoman of the company clapped him on the shoulder, saying, 'How now sir, is your hand on your halfpenny?' To whom he answered, 'No fair lady, my hand is on my heart, and yet mine heart is not in mine own hands.' Wherewithal abashed turning towards Dame Elinor he said, 'My sovereign and mistress, according to the charge of your command, and the duty that I owe you, my tongue shall bewray unto you the truth of mine intent. At this present a reward given me without desert, doth so rejoice me with continual remembrance thereof, that though my mind be occupied to think thereon, as that day nor night I can be quiet from that thought, yet the joy and pleasure which I conceive in the same is such, that I can neither be cloyed with continuance thereof, nor yet afraid, that any mishap can countervail so great a treasure. This is to me such a heaven to dwell in, as that I feed by day, and repose by night, upon the fresh record of this reward,' this (as he sayeth) he meant by the kiss that she lent him in the gallery, and by the profession of her last letters and words. Well, though this answer be somewhat misty, yet let my friend's excuse be: that taken upon the sudden he thought better to answer darkly, than to be mistrusted openly. Her second question was, what thing in this life did most grieve his heart, and disquiet his mind, whereunto he answered, that although his late rehearsed joy were incomparable, yet the greatest enemy that disturbed the same, was the privy worm of his own guilty conscience, which accused him evermore with great unworthiness: and that this was his greatest grief. The lady biting upon the bit at his cunning answers made unto these two questions, gan thus reply. 'Servant, I had thought to have touched you yet nearer with my third question, but I will refrain to attempt your patience: and now for my third demand, answer me directly in what manner this passion doth handle you? and how these contraries may hang together by any possibility of concord? for your words are strange.' F.J. now rousing himself boldly took occasion thus to handle his answer. 'Mistress,' quod he, 'my words indeed are strange, but yet my passion is much stronger, and thereupon this other day to content mine own fantasy I devised a *sonnet*, which although it be a piece of Cocklorel's music, and such as I might be ashamed to publish in this company, yet because my truth in this answer may the better appear unto you, I pray you vouchsafe to receive the same in writing,' and drawing a paper out of his pocket presented it unto her, wherein was written this sonnet.

G.T.

Love, hope, and death, do stir in me such strife,
As never man but I led such a life.
First burning love doth wound my heart to death,
And when death comes at call of inward grief
Cold lingering hope, doth feed my fainting breath,
Against my will, and yields my wound relief:
So that I live, but yet my life is such,
As death would never grieve me half so much.
No comfort then but only this I taste,
To salve such sore, such hope will never want,
And with such hope, such life will ever last,
And with such life, such sorrows are not scant.

O strange desire, o life with torments tossed
Through too much hope, mine only hope is lost.

                    Even HE   F.J.

This *sonnet* was highly commended, and in my judgement it
deserveth no less. I have heard F.J. say, that he borrowed the
invention of an Italian: but were it a translation or invention
(if I be judge) it is both pretty and pithy. His duty thus per-
formed, their pastime ended, and at their departure for a
watch word he counselled his mistress by little and little to
walk abroad, saying that the gallery near adjoining was so
pleasant, that if he were half dead he thought that by walking
therein he might be half and more revived. 'Think you so
servant?' quod she, 'and the last time I walked there I suppose
I took the cause of my malady, but by your advice (and for
you have so clearly staunched my bleeding) I will essay to
walk there tomorrow.' 'Mistress,' quod he, 'and in more full
accomplishment of my duty towards you, and in sure hope
that you will use the same only to your own private commo-
dity, will there await upon you, and between you and me will
teach you the full order how to staunch the bleeding of any
creature, whereby you shall be as cunning as myself.' 'Gra-
mercy good servant,' quod she, 'I think you lost the same in
writing here yesterday, but I cannot understand it, and there-
fore tomorrow (if I feel myself anything amended) I will send
for you thither to instruct me throughly.' Thus they parted.
And at supper time the Knight of the castle finding fault that
his guest's stomach served him no better began to accuse the
grossness of his viands, to whom one of the gentlewomen
which had passed the afternoon in his company answered,
'Nay sir,' quod she, 'this gentleman hath a passion, the which
once in a day at least doth kill his appetite.' 'Are you so well
acquainted with the disposition of his body?' quod the lord
of the house. 'By his own saying,' quod she, 'and not other-
wise.' 'Fair lady,' quod F.J., 'you either mistook me or over-
heard me then, for I told of a comfortable humour which so
fed me with continual remembrance of joy, as that my
stomach being full thereof doth desire in manner none other
victuals.' 'Why sir,' quod the lord of the house, 'do you then
live by love?' 'God forbid sir,' quod F.J., 'for then my cheeks
would be much thinner than they be, but there are divers

other greater causes of joy than the doubtful lots of love, and for mine own part, to be plain, I cannot love, and I dare not hate.' 'I would I thought so,' quod the gentlewoman. And thus with pretty nips, they passed over their supper: which ended, the lord of the house required F.J. to dance and pass the time with the gentlewoman, which he refused not to do. But suddenly, before the music was well tuned, came out Dame *Elinor* in her night attire, and said to the lord, that (supposing the solitariness of her chamber had increased her malady) she came out for her better recreation to see them dance. 'Well done daughter,' quod the lord. 'And I mistress,' quod F.J., 'would gladly bestow the leading of you about this great chamber, to drive away the faintness of your fever.' 'No good servant,' quod the lady, 'but in my stead, I pray you dance with this fair gentlewoman,' pointing him to the lady that had so taken him up at supper. F.J. to avoid mistrust, did agree to her request without furder entreaty. The dance begun, this knight marched on with the image of St. *Frances* in his mind, and St. Elinor in his heart. The violands at the end of the pavion stayed a while: in which time this dame said to F.J. on this wise. 'I am right sorry for you in two respects, although the familiarity have hitherto had no great continuance between us: and as I do lament your case, so do I rejoice (for mine own contentation) that I shall now see a due trial of the experiment which I have long desired.' This said, she kept silence. When F.J. (somewhat astonied with her strange speech) thus answered: 'Mistress although I cannot conceive the meaning of your words, yet by courtesy I am constrained to yield you thanks for your good will, the which appeareth no less in lamenting of mishaps, than in rejoicing at good fortune. What experiment you mean to try of me, I know not, but I dare assure you, that my skill in experiments is very simple.' Herewith the instruments sounded a new measure, and they passed forthwards, leaving to talk, until the noise ceased: which done, the gentlewoman replied. 'I am sorry sir, that you did erewhile, deny love and all his laws, and that in so open audience.' 'Not so,' quod F.J., 'but as the word was roundly taken, so can I readily answer it by good reason.' 'Well,' quod she, 'how if the hearers will admit no reasonable answer?' 'My reason shall yet be nevertheless,' quod he, 'in reasonable judgement.' Herewith she smiled, and he cast a glance towards Dame *Elinor* askances 'art thou pleased?'. Again the viols called them forthwards, and again at the end of the brawl said F.J. to this gentlewoman: 'I pray you mistress, and what may be the second cause of your sorrow sustained on my behalf?' 'Nay soft,' quod she, 'percase I have not yet told you the first, but content yourself, for the second cause you shall never know at my hands, until I see due trial of the experiment which I have long desired.' 'Why then,' quod he, 'I can but with a present occasion to bring the same into effect, to the end that I might also understand the mystery of your meaning.' 'And so might you fail of your purpose,' quod she, 'for I mean to be better assured of him that shall know the depth of mine intent in such a secret, than I do suppose that any creature (one except) may be of you.' 'Gentlewoman,' quod he, 'you speak *Greek*, the which I have now forgotten, and mine instructors are so far from me at this present to expound your words.' 'Or else so near,' quod she, and so smiling stayed her talk, when the music called them to another dance. Which ended, F.J. half afraid of false suspect, and more amazed at this strange talk, gave over, and bringing Mistress Frances to her place was thus saluted by his mistress. 'Servant,' quod she, 'I had done you great wrong to have danced with you, considering that this gentlewoman and you had former occasion of so weighty conference.' 'Mistress,' said F.J., 'you had done me great pleasure, for by our conference I have but brought my brains in a busy conjecture.' 'I doubt not,' said his mistress, 'but you will end that business safely.' 'It is hard,' said F.J., 'to end the thing, whereof yet I have found no beginning.' His mistress with change of countenance kept silence, whereat Dame *Frances* rejoicing, cast out this bone to gnaw upon. 'I perceive,' quod she, 'it is evil to halt before a cripple.' F.J. perceiving now that his mistress waxed angry, thought good on her behalf thus to answer: 'And it is evil to hop before them that run for the bell': his mistress replied, 'And it is evil to hang the bell at their heels which are always running.' The lord of the castle overhearing these proper quips, rose out of his chair, and coming towards F.J. required him to dance a galliard. 'Sir,' said F.J., 'I have hitherto at your appointment but walked about the house, now if you be desirous to see one tumble a turn or twain, it is like enough that I might provoke you to laugh at me, but in good faith my dancing days are almost done, and therefore sir,' quod he, 'I pray you speak to them that are more nimble at tripping on the toe.' Whilst he was thus saying Dame Elinor had made her *congé*, and was now entering the door of her chamber: when F.J. all amazed at her sudden departure followed her to take leave of his mistress: but she more than angry, refused to hear his good night, and entering her chamber caused her maid to clap the door. F.J. with heavy cheer returned to his company, and Mistress *Frances* to touch his sore with a corrosive said to him softly in this wise, 'Sir you may now perceive that this our country cannot allow the French manner of dancing, for they (as I have heard tell) do more commonly dance to talk, than entreat to dance.' F.J. hoping to drive out one nail with another, and thinking this a mean almost convenient to suppress all jealous supposes took Mistress *Frances* by the hand and with a heavy smile answered. 'Mistress and I (because I have seen the French manner of dancing) will eftsoons entreat you to dance a bargynet.' 'What mean you by this?' quod Mistress Frances. 'If it please you to follow,' quod he, 'you shall see that I can jest without joy and laugh without lust,' and calling the musicians, caused them softly to sound the tintarnell, when he clearing his voice did *alla Napolitana* apply these verses following unto the measure.

G.T.

In prime of lusty years, when Cupid caught me in
And nature taught the way to love, how I might best begin:
To please my wand'ring eye, in beauty's tickle trade,
To gaze on each that passed by, a careless sport I made.

With sweet enticing bait, I fished for many a dame,
And warmed me by many a fire, yet felt I not the flame:
But when at last I spied, the face that pleased me most,
The coals were quick, the wood was dry, and I began to toast.

And smiling yet full oft, I have beheld that face
When in my heart I might bewail mine own unlucky case:
And oft again with looks that might bewray my grief,
I pleaded hard for just reward, and fought to find relief.

107

What will you move? so oft, my gazing eyes did seek
To see the rose and lily strive upon that lively cheek:
Till at the last I spied, and by good proof I found,
That in that face was painted plain, the piercer of my wound.

Then (all too late) aghast, I did my foot retire,
And sought with secret sighs to quench my greedy scalding
    fire:
But lo, I did prevail as much to guide my will,
As he that seeks with halting heel, to hop against the bill.

Or as the feeble sight, would search the sunny beam,
Even so I found but labour lost, to strive against the stream.
Then gan I thus resolve, since liking forced love,
Should I mislike my happy choice, before I did it prove?

And since none other joy I had but her to see,
Should I retire my deep desire? no no it would not be:
Though great to duty were, that she did well deserve,
And I poor man, unworthy am so worthy a wight to serve,

Yet hope my comfort stayed, that she would have regard
To my good will, that nothing craved, but like for just reward:
I see the falcon gent sometimes will take delight,
To seek the solace of her wing, and dally with a kite.

The fairest wolf will choose the foulest for her make,
And why? because he doth endure most sorrow for her sake
Even so had I like hope, when doleful days were spent
When weary words were wasted well, to open true intent.

When floods of flowing tears, had washed my weeping eyes,
When trembling tongue had troubled her, with loud lamenting
    cries,
At last her worthy will would pity this my plaint,
And comfort me her own poor slave, whom fear had made so
    faint.

Wherefore I made a vow, the stony rock should start,
Ere I presume, to let her slip out of my faithful heart.

L'envoy
And when she saw by proof, the pith of my good will,
She took in worth this simple song, for want of better skill:
And as my just deserts, her gentle heart did move,
She was content to answer thus: I am content to love.

F.J.

These verses are more in number than do stand with conten-
tation of some judgements, and yet the occasion thoroughly
considered, I can commend them with the rest, for it is (as may
be well termed) *continua oratio*, declaring a full discourse of
his first love: wherein (over and beside that the epithets are
aptly applied, and the verse of itself pleasant enough) I note
that by it he meant in clouds to decipher into Mistress *Frances*
such matter as she would snatch at, and yet could take no
good hold of the same. Furthermore, it answered very aptly
to the note which the music sounded, as the skilful reader by
due trial may approve. This singing, or dancing song ended,
Mistress *Frances* giving due thanks, seemed weary also of the
company, and proffering to depart, gave yet this farewell to
F.J. not vexed by choler, but pleased with contention, and
called away by heavy sleep: 'I am constrained,' quod she, 'to
bid you good night,' and so turning to the rest of the company,
took her leave. Then the master of the house commanded a
torch to light F.J. to his lodging, where (as I have heard him
say) the sudden change of his mistress' countenance, together
with the strangeness of Mistress *Frances*' talk, made such an
encounter in his mind, that he could take no rest that night:
wherefore in the morning rising very early (although it were
far before his Mistress' hour) he cooled his choler by walking
in the gallery near to her lodging, and there in this passion
compiled these verses following.

G.T.

A cloud of care hath covered all my coast,
And storms of strife do threaten to appear:
The waves of woe, which I mistrusted most,
Have broke the banks wherein my life lay clear:
Chips of ill chance, are fallen amid my choice,
To mar the mind, that meant for to rejoice.

Before I sought, I found the haven of hap,
Wherein (once found) I sought to shroud my ship,
But lowering love hath lift me from her lap,
And crabbed lot begins to hang the lip:
The drops of dark mistrust do fall so thick,
They pierce my coat, and touch my skin at quick.

What may be said, where truth cannot prevail?
What plea may serve, where will itself is judge?
What reason rules, where right and reason fail?
Remediless then must the guiltless trudge:
And seek out care, to be the carving knife
To cut the thread, that ling'reth such a life.

F.J.

This is but a rough metre, and reason, for it was devised in great disquiet of mind, and written in rage, yet have I seen much worse pass the musters, yea and where both the Lieutenant and Provost Marshal were men of ripe judgement: and as it is, I pray you let it pass here, for the truth is that F.J. himself had so slender liking thereof, or at least of one word escaped therein, that he never presented it, but to the matter. When he had long (and all in vain) looked for the coming of his mistress into her appointed walk: he wandered into the park near adjoining to the castle wall, where his chance was to meet Mistress *Frances*, accompanied with one other gentlewoman, by whom he passed with a reverence of courtesy: and so walking on, came into the side of a thicket, where he sat down under a tree to allay his sadness with solitariness. Mistress *Frances*, partly of courtesy and affection, and partly to content her mind by continuance of such talk as they had commenced overnight, entreated her companion to go with her unto this tree of reformation, whereas they found the knight with his arms unfolded in a heavy kind of contemplation, unto whom Mistress *Frances* stepped apace (right softly) and at unawares gave this salutation. 'I little thought sir knight,' quod she, 'by your evensong yesternight, to have found you presently at such a morrow mass, but I perceive you serve your saint with double devotion: and I pray God grant you treble meed for your good intent.' F.J. taken thus upon the sudden, could none otherwise answer but thus: 'I told you mistress,' quod he, 'that I could laugh without lust, and jest without joy:' and therewithal starting up, with a more bold countenance came towards the dame, proffering unto them his service, to wait upon them homewards. 'I have heard you say oft times,' quod *Frances*, 'that it is hard to serve two masters at one time, but we will be right glad of your company.' 'I thank you,' quod *F.J.*, and so walking with them, fell into sundry discourses, still refusing to touch any part of their former communication, until Mistress *Frances* said unto him: 'By my troth,' quod she, 'I would be your debtor these two days, to answer me truly but unto one question that I will command.' 'Fair gentlewoman,' quod he, 'you shall not need to become my debtor, but if it please you to quit question by question, I will be more ready to gratify you in this request, than either reason requireth, or than you would be willing to work my contentation.' 'Master *F.J.*,' quod she and that sadly, 'peradventure you know but a little how willing I would be to procure your contentation, but you know that hitherto familiarity hath taken no deep root between us twain. And though I find in you no manner of cause whereby I might doubt to commit this or greater matter unto you, yet have I stayed hitherto so to do, in doubt lest you might thereby justly condemn me both of arrogancy and lack of discretion, wherewith I must yet foolishly affirm, that I have with great pain bridled my tongue from disclosing the same unto you. Such is then the good will that I bear towards you, the which if you rather judge to be impudence, than a friendly meaning, I may then curse the hour that I first concluded thus to deal with you.' Herewithal being now red for chaste bashfulness, she abased her eyes, and stayed her talk, to whom *F.J.* thus answered. 'Mistress *Frances*, if I should with so exceeding villainy requite such and so exceeding courtesy, I might not only seem to degenerate from all gentry, but also to differ in behaviour from all the rest of my life spent: wherefore to be plain with you in few words, I think myself so bound unto you for divers respects, as if ability do not fail me, you shall find me mindful in requital of the same: and for disclosing your mind to me, you may if so please you adventure without adventure, for by this sun,' quod he, 'I will not deceive such trust as you shall lay upon me, and furthermore, so far as I may, I will be yours in any respect: wherefore I beseech

111

you accept me for your faithful friend, and so shall you surely find me.' 'Not so,' quod she, 'but you shall be my *Trust*, if you vouchsafe the name, and I will be to you as you shall please to term me.' 'My *Hope*,' quod he, 'if you will be pleased,' and thus agreed, they two walked apart from the other gentlewoman, and fell into sad talk, wherein Mistress *Frances* did very courteously declare unto him, that indeed, one cause of her sorrow sustained in his behalf, was that he had said so openly overnight, that he could not love, for she perceived very well the affection between him and Madam *Elinor*, and she was also advertised that Madam *Elinor* stood in the portal of her chamber, hearkening to the talk they had at supper that night, wherefore she seemed to be sorry that such a word (rashly escaped) might become great hindrance unto his desire: but a greater cause of her grief was (as she declared) that his hap was to bestow his liking so unworthily, for she seemed to accuse Dame *Elinor*, for the most inconstant woman living: in full proof whereof, she bewrayed unto *F.J.* how the same Dame *Elinor* had of long time been yielded to the minion *secretary*, whom I have before described: in whom though there be (quod she) no one point of worthiness, yet shamed she not to use him as her dearest friend, or rather her holiest idol, and that this not withstanding Dame *Elinor* had been also sundry times won to choice of change, as she named unto *F.J.* two gentlemen whereof the one was named *H.D.* and that other *H.K.* by whom she was during sundry times of their several abode in those parts, entreated to like courtesy, for these causes the Dame *Frances* seemed to mislike F.J.'s choice, and to lament that she doubted in process of time to see him abused.

The experiment she meant was this, for that she thought *F.J.* (I use her words) a man in every respect worthy to have the use of a more commodious common, she hoped now to see if his enclosure thereof might be defensible against her said secretary, and such like. These things and divers other of great importance, this courteous lady *Frances* did friendly disclose unto *F.J.* and furthermore, did both instruct and advise him how to proceed in his enterprise. Now to make my talk good, and lest the reader might be drawn in a jealous suppose of this lady *Frances*, I must let you understand that she was unto *F.J.* a kinswoman, a virgin of rare chastity,

112

singular capacity, notable modesty, and excellent beauty: and though *F.J.* had cast his affection on the other (being a married woman) yet was there in their beauties no great difference: but in all other gifts a wonderful diversity, as much as might be between constancy and flitting fantasy, between womanly countenance and girlish garishness, between hot dissimulation and temperate fidelity. Now if any man will curiously ask the question why *F.J.* should choose the one and leave the other, over and besides the common proverb? (So many men, so many minds) thus may be answered: we see by common experience, that the highest flying falcon, doth most commonly prey upon the corn-fed crow, and the simple shiftless dove, than on the mounting kite: and why? Because the one is overcome with less difficulty than the other. Thus much in defence of the Lady *Frances*, and to excuse the choice of my friend *F.J.* who thought himself now no less beholding to good fortune, to have found such a trusty friend, than bounden to Dame *Venus*, to have won such a mistress. And to return unto my pretence, understand you, that *F.J.* (being now with these two fair ladies come very near the castle) grew in some jealous doubt (as on his own behalf) whether he were best to break company or not. When his assured *Hope*, perceiving the same, gan thus re-comfort him: 'Good sir,' quod she, 'if you trusted your trusty friends, you should not need thus cowardly to stand in dread of your deadly enemies.' 'Well said in faith,' quod *F.J.*, 'and I must confess, you were in my bosom before I wist, but yet I have heard said often, that in *Trust* is treason.' 'Well spoken for yourself,' quod his *Hope*. *F.J.* now remembering that he had but erstwhile taken him the name of her *Trust*, came home *per misericordiam*, when his *Hope* entering the castle gate, caught hold of his lap, and half by force led him by the gallery unto his mistress' chamber: whereas after a little dissembling disdain, he was at last by the good help of his *Hope*, right thankfully received: and for his mistress was now ready to dine, he was therefore for that time arrested there, and a *supersedias* sent into the great chamber unto the lord of the house, who expected his coming out of the park. The dinner ended, and he thoroughly contented both with welfare and welcome, they fell into sundry devices of pastime: at last *F.J.* taking into his hand a lute that lay upon his mistress' bed, did unto the note of the *Venetian* galliard apply the Italian

113

ditty written by the worthy *Bradamant* unto the noble *Rugier*, as *Ariosto* hath it, *Rugier qual semper fui, etc*. but his mistress would not be quiet until she heard him repeat the *Tyntarnell* which he had used overnight, the which *F.J.* refused not, and end whereof his mistress thinking now she had showed herself too earnest to use any further dissimulation, especially perceiving the forward inclination of her servant's *Hope*, fell to flat plain dealing, and walking to the window, called her servant apart unto her, of whom she demanded secretly and in sad earnest, who devised this *Tyntarnell*? 'My father's sister's brother's son,' quod F.J. His mistress laughing right heartily, demanded yet again, by whom the same was figured: 'By a niece to an aunt of yours, mistress,' quod he. 'Well then servant,' quod she, 'I swear unto you here by my father's soul, that my mother's youngest daughter, doth love your father's eldest son, above any creature living.' *F.J.* hereby recomforted, gan thus reply. 'Mistress, though my father's eldest son be far unworthy of so noble a match, yet since it pleaseth her so well to accept him, I would thus much say behind his back, that your mother's daughter hath done him some wrong.' 'And wherein, servant?' quod she. 'By my troth, mistress,' quod he, 'it is not yet xx hours, since without touch of breast she gave him such a nip by the heart, as did altogether bereave him his night's rest, with the bruise thereof.' 'Well servant,' quod she, 'content yourself, and for your sake, I will speak to her to provide him a plaster, the which I myself will apply to his hurt: and to the end it may work the better with him, I will purvey a lodging for him, where hereafter he may sleep at more quiet.'

Thus said the rosy hue, distained her sickly cheeks, and she returned to the company, leaving *F.J.* ravished between hope and dread, as one that could neither conjecture the meaning of her mystical words, nor assuredly trust unto the knot of her sliding affections. When the Lady *Frances* coming to him, demanded, 'What, dream you sir?' 'Yea marry do I fair lady,' quod he. 'I dreamed,' quod *F.J.*, 'that walking in a pleasant garden garnished with sundry delights, my hap was to espy hanging in the air, a hope wherein I might well behold the aspects and face of the heavens, and calling to remembrance the day and hour of my nativity, I did thereby (according to my small skill in astronomy) try the conclusions of mine

114

adventures.' 'And what found you therein?' quod Dame *Frances*. 'You awaked me out of my dream,' quod he, 'or else peradventure you should not have known.' 'I believe you well,' quod the *Lady Frances*, and laughing at his quick answer brought him by the hand unto the rest of his company: where he tarried not long before his gracious mistress bad him farewell, and to keep his bower there again, when he should by her be summoned. Hereby *F.J.* passed the rest of that day in hope awaiting the happy time when his mistress should send for him. Suppertime came and passed over, and not long after came the handmaid of the Lady *Elinor* into the great chamber, desiring *F.J.* to repair unto their mistress, the which he willingly accomplished: and being now entered into her chamber, he might perceive his mistress in her night's attire, preparing herself towards bed, to whom *F.J.* said: 'Why how now Mistress? I had thought this night to have seen you dance (at least or at last) amongst us?' 'By my troth good servant,' quod she, 'I adventured so soon unto the great chamber yesternight, that I find myself somewhat sickly disposed and therefore do strain courtesy (as you see) to go the sooner to my bed this night: but before I sleep,' quod she, 'I am to charge you with a matter of weight,' and taking him apart from the rest, declared that (as that present night) she would talk with him more at large in the gallery adjoining to her chamber. Hereupon *F.J.* discreetly dissimulating his joy, took his leave and retired into the great chamber, where he had not long continued before the Lord of the castle commanded a torch to light him to his lodging, whereas as he prepared himself and went to bed, commanding his servant also to go to his rest. And when he thought his servant, as the rest of the household be safe, he arose again, and taking his nightgown, did under the same convey his naked sword, and so walked to the gallery, where he found his good mistress walking in her nightgown and attending his coming. The moon was now at the full, the skies clear, and the weather temperate, by reason whereof he might the more plainly, and with the greater contentation behold his long desired joys, and spreading his arms abroad to embrace his loving mistress, he said: 'Oh my dear lady when shall I be able with the least desert to countervail the least part of this your bountiful goodness?' The dame (whether it were of fear indeed, or that

115

the wiliness of womanhood had taught her to cover her conceits with some fine dissimulation) start back from the knight, and shrieking (but softly) said unto him, 'Alas servant what have I deserved, that you come against me with naked sword as against an open enemy.' *F.J.* perceiving her intent excused himself, declaring that he brought the same for their defence, and not to offend her in any wise. The lady being therewith somewhat appeased, they began with more comfortable gesture to expel the dread of the said late affright, and sithence to become bolder of behaviour, more familiar in speech, and most kind in accomplishing of common comfort. But why hold I so long discourse in describing the joys which (for lack of like experience) I cannot set out to the full? Were it not that I know to whom I write, I would the more beware what I write. *F.J.* was a man, and neither of us are senseless, and therefore I should slander him (over and besides a greater obloquy to the whole genealogy of *Aeneas*) if I should imagine that of tender heart he would forbear to express her more tender limbs against the hard floor. Suffice that of her courteous nature she was content to accept boards for a bed of down, mats for cameric sheets, and the nightgown of *F.J.* for a counterpoint to cover them, and thus with calm content, in stead of quiet sleep, they beguiled the night, until the proudest star began to abandon the firmament, when *F.J.* and his mistress, were constrained also to abandon their delights, and with ten thousand sweet kisses and straight embracings, did frame themselves to play loth to depart. Well, remedy was there none, but Dame *Elinor* must return unto her chamber, and *F.J.* must also convey himself (as closely as might be) into his chamber, the which was hard to do, the day being so far sprung, and he having a large base court to pass over before he could recover his stairfoot door. And though he were not much perceived, yet the Lady *Frances* being no less desirous to see an issue to these enterprises, than *F.J.* was to cover them in secrecy, did watch, and even at the entering of his chamber door, perceived the point of his naked sword glistering under the skirt of his nightgown: whereat she smiled and said to herself, this gear goeth well about. Well, *F.J.* having now recovered his chamber, he went to bed, and there let him sleep, as his mistress did on that other side. Although the Lady *Frances* being throughly tickled now in

116

all the veins, could not enjoy such quiet rest, but arising, took another gentlewoman of the house with her, and walked into the park to take the fresh air of the morning. They had not long walked there, but they returned, and though *F.J.* had not yet slept sufficiently, for one who had so far travailed in the night past, yet they went into his chamber to raise him, and coming to his bedside, found him fast on sleep. 'Alas,' quod that other gentlewoman, 'it were pity to wake him.' 'Even so it were,' quod Dame *Frances*, 'but we will take away somewhat of his, whereby he may perceive that we were here,' and looking about his chamber, his naked sword presented itself into the hands of Dame *Frances*, who took it with her, and softly shutting his chamber door again, went down the stairs and recovered her own lodging, in good order and unperceived of anybody, saving only that other gentlewoman which accompanied her. At the last *F.J.* awaked, and apparelling himself, walked out also to take the air, and being thoroughly recomforted as well with remembrance of his joys forepassed, as also with the pleasant harmony which the birds made on every side, and the fragrant smell of the redolent flowers and blossoms which budded on every branch, he did in these delights compile these verses following.

The occasion (as I have heard him rehearse) was by encounter that he had with his lady by light of the moon: and forasmuch, as the moon in midst of their delights did vanish away, or was overspread with a cloud, thereupon he took the subject of his theme. And thus it ensueth, called A Moonshine Banquet.

G.T.

Dame Cynthia herself (that shines so bright,
And deigneth not to leave her lofty place:
But only then, when Phoebus shows his face
Which is her brother born and tends her light,)
Disdained not yet to do my lady right:
To prove that in such heavenly wights as she,
It fitteth best that right and reason be.
For when she spied my lady's golden rays,
Into the clouds,
Her head she shrouds,
And shamed to shine where she her beams displays.

Good reason yet, that to my simple skill,
I should the name of Cynthia adore:
By whose high help, I might behold the more
My lady's lovely looks at mine own will,
With deep content, to gare, and gaze my fill:
Of courtesy and not of dark disdain,
Dame Cynthia disclosed my lady plain.
She did but lend her light (as for a light)
With friendly grace,
To show her face,
That else would show and shine in her despite.

Dan Phoebus he with many a lowering look,
Had her beheld of yore in angry wise:
And when he could none other mean devise
To stain her name, this deep deceit he took
To be the bait that best might hide his hook:
Into her eyes his parching beams he cast,
To scorch their skins, that gazed in her full fast:
Whereby when many a man was sunburnt so
They thought my Queen,
The sun had been
With scalding flames, which wrought them all their woe.

And thus when many a look had looked so long,
As that their eyes were dim and dazzled both:
Some fainting hearts that were both lewd and loth
To look again from whence the error sprung,
Gan close their eye from fear of further wrong:
And some again once drawn into the maze,
Gan lewdly blame the beams of beauty's blaze:
But I with deep foresight did soon espy,
How Phoebus meant,
By false intent,
To slander to her name with cruelty.

Wherefore at better leisure thought I best,
To try the treason of his treachery:
And to exalt my lady's dignity
When Phoebus fled and drew him down to rest
Amid the waves that walter in the west,

118

I gan behold this lovely lady's face,
Whereon Dame Nature spent her gifts of grace:
And found therein no parching heat at all,
But such bright hue,
As might renew,
An angel's joys in reign celestial.

The courteous moon that wished to do me good,
Did shine to show my dame more perfectly,
But when she saw her passing jollity,
The moon for shame, did blush as red as blood,
And shrunk aside and kept her horns in hood:
So that now when Dame Cynthia was gone,
I might enjoy my lady's looks alone,
Yet honoured still the moon with true intent:
Who taught us skill,
To work our will,
And gave us place, till all the night was spent.

F.J.

This ballade, or howsoever I shall term it, percase you will
not like, and yet in my judgement it hath great good store
of deep invention, and for the order of the verse, it is not
common, I have not heard many of like proportion, some
will account it but a diddledum: but whoso hath heard
F.J. sing it to the lute, by a note of his own device, I suppose
he would esteem it a pleasant diddledum, and for my part,
if I were not partial, I would say more in commendation
of it than now I mean to do, leaving it to you and like
judgements . . .

[F.J., Frances and Elinor go riding together; but he is anxious
about his missing sword. Elinor rescues it for him. He visits
her one Friday morning, and writes a sonnet for her he calls
'A Friday's Breakfast'; and a much longer challenge to Beauty,
beginning: 'Beauty shut up thy shop, and truss up all thy
trash,/My Nell hath stolen thy finest stuff, & left thee in the
lash.' The vein of praise is furthered by a sonnet translated
from the Italian.

Elinor's husband returns; F.J. coolly goes hunting with
him. What really perturbs him is the return of the secretary.

119

He takes to his bed. The ladies visit him, and Elinor's courtesies ease his mind for a while before suspicion returns. The ladies return with a perfumed pillow and a game, in which F.J. has to act as 'governor' to settle various questions. He answers one long case of love and desertion from the old experienced courtier Madam Pergo. Elinor returns, alone, later; but F.J. is too frank about his suspicions, and they row in bed. She gets together with the secretary again. Frances tries to take over the nurse's role. She gives him another, pointed, case for the game, of an adulterous wife and her husband.]

. . . the lot fell on Dame *Frances* to propound the second question, who addressing her speech unto *F.J.* said in this wise, 'Noble governor, I will rehearse unto you a strange history, not feigned, neither borrowed out of any old authority, but a thing done indeed of late days, and not far distant from this place where we now remain. It chanced that a gentleman our neighbour being married to a very fair gentlewoman, lived with her by the space of four or five years in great contentation, trusting her no less than he loved her, and yet loving her as much as any man could love a woman. On that other side the gentleman had won (unto her beauty) a singular commendation for her chaste and modest behaviour. Yet it happened in time that a lusty young gentleman (who very often resorted to them) obtained that at her hands, which never any man could before him attain: and to be plain, he won so much in her affections, that forgetting both her duty and her husband's kindness, she yielded her body at the commandment of this lover, in which pastime they passed long time by their politic government. At last the friends of this lady (and especially three sisters which she had) espied overmuch familiarity between the two lovers, and dreading lest it might break out to their common reproach took their sister apart, and declared that the world did judge scarce well of the repair of that gentleman unto her house: and that if she did not foresee it in time, she should not only lose the good credit which she herself had hitherto possessed, but furthermore should distain their whole race with obloquy and reproach. These and sundry other goodly admonitions of these sisters could not sink in the mind of this gentlewoman, for she did not only stand in defiance of what any man could

120

think of her, but also seemed to accuse them, that because they saw her estimation (being their younger) to grow about their own, they had therefore devised this mean to set variance between her husband and her. The sisters seeing their wholesome counsel so rejected, and her continue still in obstinate opinion, addressed their speech unto her husband, declaring that the world judged not the best, neither they themselves did very well like of the familiarity between their sister and that gentleman, and therefore advised him to forecast all perils, and in time to forbid him his house. The husband (on that other side) had also conceived such a good opinion of his guest, and had growen into such a strict familiarity with him, that you might with more ease have removed a stone wall, than once to make him think amiss, either of his wife, or of her lover: yea and immediately after this conference he would not stick thus to say unto his wife. '*Bess*,' (for so indeed was her name) 'thou hast three such busy brained sisters, as I think shortly their heads will break: they would have me to be jealous of thee, no no Bess etc.' so that he was not only far from any such belief, but furthermore did every day increase his courtesies towards the lover. The sisters being thus on all sides rejected, and yet perceiving more and more an unseemly behaviour between their sister and her minion, began to melt in their own grease: and such was their enraged pretence of revenge, that they suborned divers servants in the house to watch so diligently, as that this treason might be discovered. Amongst the rest, one maybe of subtle spirit had so long watched them, that at last she espied them go into a chamber together, and lock the door to them: whereupon she ran with all haste possible to her master, and told him that if he would come with her, she would show him a very strange sight. The gentleman (suspecting nothing) went with her until he came into a chamber near unto that wherein they had shut themselves, and she pointing her master to the keyhole, bad him look through, where he saw the thing which most might mislike him to behold. Whereat he suddenly drew his dagger, and turned towards the maid, who fled from him for fear of mischief: but when he could not overtake her in the heat of his choler, he commanded that she should forthwith truss up that little which she had and to depart his service: and before her departure he found means to talk with

121

her, threatening that if ever she spake any word of this mystery in any place where she should come, it should cost her life. The maid for fear departed in silence, and the master never changed countenance either to his wife or to her paramour, but feigned unto his wife that he had turned away the maid upon that sudden, for that she had thrown a kitchen knife at him, whiles he went about to correct a fault in her etc. Thus the good gentleman drank up his own sweat unseen every day, increasing courtesy to the lover, and never changing countenance to his wife in anything, but only that he refrained to have such knowledge of her carnally as he in times past had, and other men have of their wives. In this sort he continued by the space of half a year, nevertheless lamenting his mishap in solitary places. At last (what moved him I know not) he fell again to company with his wife as other men do, and as I have heard it said he used this policy: every time that he had knowledge of her, he would leave in the bed, or in some place where she must needs find it, a piece of money which then was fallen to three halfpence: and I remember they called them slips. Thus he dealt with her continually by the space of four or five months, using her nevertheless very kindly in all other respects, and providing for her all things necessary at the first call: but unto his guest he still augmented courtesy, in such sort, that you would have thought them to be sworn brothers. All this notwithstanding his wife much musing at these three halfpenny pieces which she found in this sort, and furthermore, having sundry times found her husband in solitary places making great lamentation, she grew inquisitive, what should be the secret cause of these alterations: unto whom he would none otherwise answer, but that any man should find occasion to be more pensive at one time than at another. The wife notwithstanding increasing her suspect, emported the same unto her lover, alleging therewithal that she doubted very much lest her husband had some vehement suspicion of their affairs. The lover encouraged her, and likewise declared, that if she would be importunate to enquire the cause, her husband would not be able to keep it from her: and having now throughly instructed her, she dealt with her husband in this sort. One day when she knew him to be in his study alone, she came unto him, and having fast locked the door after her, and conveyed the key into her pocket, she

122

began first with earnest entreaty, and then with tears to crave that he would no longer keep from her the cause of his sudden alteration. The husband dissimuled the matter still: at last she was so earnest to know for what cause he left money in such sort at sundry times, that he answered in this wise: 'Wife,' quod he, 'thou knowest how long we have been married together, and how long I made so dear account of thee as ever man made of his wife: since which days, thou knowest also how long I refrained thy company, and how long again I have used thy company leaving the money in this sort, and the cause is this. So long as thou didst behave thyself faithfully towards me, I never loathed thy company, but sithence I have perceived thee to be a harlot, and therefore did I for long time refrain and forbear to lie with thee: and now I can no longer forbear it, I do give thee every time I lie with thee a slip, which is to make thee understand thine own whoredom: and this reward is sufficient for a whore.' The wife began to stand stoutly at defiance, but the husband cut off her speech and declared when, where, and how he had seen it: hereat the woman being abashed, and finding her conscience guilty of as much as he had alleged, fell down on her knees, and with most bitter tears craved pardon, confessing her offence: whereat her husband (moved with pity) and melting likewise in floods of lamentation, recomforted her promising that if from that day forwards she would be true unto him, he would not only forgive all that was past, but become more tender and loving to her than ever he was. What do I tarry so long? They became of accord: and in full accomplishment thereof, the gentlewoman did altogether eschew the company, the speech, and (as much as in her lay) the sight of her lover, although her husband did continue his courtesy towards him, and often charged his wife to make him fair semblant. The lover was now only left in perplexity, who knew nothing what might be the cause of all these changes, and that most grieved him, he could by no means obtain again the speech of his desired: he watched all opportunities, he suborned messengers, he wrote letters, but all in vain. In the end she caused to be declared to him a time and a place where she would meet him and speak with him. Being met, she put him in remembrance of all that had passed between them: she laid also before him how trusty she had been unto him in all professions: she confessed also how faithfully he had discharged the duty of a friend in all respects, and therewithal she declared that her late alteration and pensiveness of mind was not without great cause, for that she had of late such a mishap, as might change the disposition of any living creature: yea and that the case was such, as unless she found present remedy, her death must needs ensue, and that speedily: for the preventing whereof, she alleged that she had beaten her brains with all device possible, and that in the end she could think of no redress but one, the which lay only in him to accomplish. Wherefore she besought him for all the love and good will which passed between them, now to show the fruits of true friendship, and to gratify her with a free grant to this request. The lover who had always been desirous to pleasure her in anything, but now especially to recover his wonted kindness, gan frankly promise to accomplish anything that might be to him possible, yea though it were to his great detriment: and therewithal did deeply blame her in that she would so long torment herself with any grief, considering that it lay in him to help it. The lady answered, that she had so long kept it from his knowledge, because she doubted whether he would be contented to perform it or not, although it was such a thing as he might safely grant without any manner of hurt to himself: and yet that now in the end she was forced to adventure upon his courtesy, being no longer able to bear the burden of her grief the lover solicited her most earnestly to disclose it: and she (as fast) seemed to mistrust that he would not accomplish it. The lover mistrusting nothing less than that ensued, took the oath willingly: which done she declared all that had passed between her and her husband: his grief, her repentance, his pardon, her vow, and in the end of her tale enjoined the lover, that from henceforthwards, he should never attempt to break her constant determination: the lover replied that this was unpossible: but she plainly assured him, that if he granted her that request, she would be his friend in all honest and goodly wise: if not, she put him out of doubt that she would eschew his company and fly from his sight as from a scorpion. The lover considering that her request was but just, accusing his own guilty conscience, remembering the great courtesies always used by her husband, and therewithal seeing the case now brought to such an issue, as that by none other means than by this it

124

could be concealed from the knowledge of the world: but most of all, being urged by his oath, did at last give an unwilling consent, and yet a faithful promise to yield unto her will in all things: and thus being become of one assent, he remaineth the dearest friend and most welcome guest that may be, both to the lady, and her husband, and the man and wife so kind (each to other) as if there never had been such a breach between them. Now, of you noble governor, I would fain learn, whether the perplexity of the husband when he looked in at the keyhole, or of the wife when she knew the cause why the slips were so scattered, or of the lover when he knew what was the mistress' charge, was greater of the three? I might have put in also the troubled thoughts of the sisters and the maid, when they saw their good will rejected, but let these three suffice.'

'Gentle *Hope*,' quod F.J., 'you have rehearsed (and that right eloquently) a notable tale, or rather a notable history, because you seem to affirm, that it was done indeed of late, and not far hence. Wherein I note five especial points: that is a marvellous patience in the husband, no less repentance in the wife, no small boldness of the maid, but much more rashness in the sisters, and last of all, a rare tractability in the lover. Nevertheless to return to your question, I think the husband's perplexity greatest, because his losses abounded above the rest, and his injuries were uncomparable.'

The Lady *Frances* did not seem to contray him, but rather smiled in her sleeve at Dame *Pergo*, who had no less patience to hear the tale recited, than the Lady *Frances* had pleasure in telling of it, but I may not rehearse the cause why, unless I should tell all. By this time the sleeping hour approached, and the ladies prepared their departure, when as Mistress *Frances* said unto *F.J.*, 'Although percase I shall not do it so handsomely as your mistress, yet good *Truth*,' quod she, 'if you vouchsafe it, I can be content to trim up your bed in the best manner that I may, as one who would be as glad as she to procure your quiet rest.' *F.J.* gave her great thanks desiring her not to trouble herself, but to let his man alone with that charge: thus they departed, and how all parties took best that night I know not: but in the morning *F.J.* began to consider with himself that he might lie long enough in his bed before his mistress would be appeased in her peevish conceits. . . .

[Still, he recovers, but Elinor leaves for another town. On her return they make up, but she is so long in responding he has to write to her requesting another moonshine banquet or Friday breakfast. She replies . . .]

I can but smile at your simplicity, who burden your friends with an impossibility. The case so stood as I could not though I would. Wherefore from henceforth either learn to frame your request more reasonably, or else stand content with a flat repulse.

SHE

F.J. liked this letter but a little: and being thereby driven into his accustomed vein, he compiled in verse this answer following, upon these words contained in her letter, *I could not though I would.*

G.T.

I could not though I would: good lady say not so,
Since one good word of your good will might soon redress my
    woe.
Where would is free before, there could can never fail:
For proof, you see how galleys pass when ships can bear no
    sail.
The weary mariner when skies are overcast,
By ready will doth guide his skill and wins the haven at last.
The pretty bird that sings with prick against her breast,
Doth make a virtue of her need to watch when others rest.
And true the proverb is which you have laid apart,
There is no hap can seem too hard unto a willing heart.
Then lovely lady mine, you say not as you should,
In doubtful terms to answer thus: I could not though I would.
Yes, yes, full well you know, your can is quick and good:
And wilful will is eke too swift to shed my guiltless blood.
But if good will were bent as pressed as power is,
Such will would quickly find the skill to mend that is amiss.
Wherefore if you desire to see my true love spilt,
Command and I will slay myself, that yours may be the guilt.
But if you have no power to say your servant nay,
Write thus: I may not as I would, yet must I as I may.

F.J.

126

Thus *F.J.* replied upon his mistress' answer, hoping thereby to recover some favour at her hands, but it would not be: so that now he had been as likely (as at the first) to have fretted in fantasies, had not the Lady *Frances* continually comforted him: and by little and little she drove such reason into his mind, that now he began to subdue his humours with discretion, and to determine that if he might espy evident proof of his mistress' frailty, he would then stand content with patience perforce, and give his mistress the *bezo las manos*. And it happened one day amongst others, that he resorted to his mistress' chamber and found her (*allo solito*) lying upon her bed, and the secretary with Dame *Pergo* and her handmaid keeping of her company. Whereat *F.J.* somewhat refining, came to her and fell to dalliance, as one that had now rather adventure to be thought presumptuous than yield to be accounted bashful, he cast his arm over his mistress, and began to accuse her of sluggishness, using some other bold parts, as well to provoke her, as also to grieve the other. The lady seemed little to delight in his dallying, but cast a glance at her secretary and therewith smiled, when as the secretary and Dame *Pergo* burst out into open laughter. The which *F.J.* perceiving, and disdaining her ingratitude, was forced to depart, and in that fantasy compiled this sonnet.

G.T.

With her in arms that had my heart in hold,
I stood of late to plead for pity so:
And as I did her lovely looks behold,
She cast a glance upon my rival foe.
His fleering face provoked her to smile,
When my salt tears were drowned in disdain:
He glad, I sad, he laughed (alas the while)
I wept for woe: I pined for deadly pain.
And when I saw none other boot prevail,
But reason's rule must guide my skilful mind:
Why then (quod I) old proverbs never fail,
For yet was never good cat out of kind:
Nor women true but even as stories tell,
Won with an egg, and lost again with shell.

F.J.

This sonnet declareth that he began now to account of her as she deserved, for it hath a sharp conclusion, and it is some-what too general. Well, as it is he lost it where his mistress found it, and she immediately imparted the same unto Dame *Pergo*, and Dame *Pergo* unto others: so that it quickly became common in the house. Amongst others Mistress *Frances* having a copy of it, did seem to pardon the generality, and to be well pleased with the particularity thereof, the which she bewrayed unto *F.J.* in this wise. 'Of all the joys that ever I had, my good *Trust*,' quod she, 'there is none wherein I take more comfort than in your conformity, and although your present rage is such that you can be content to condemn a number unknown, for the transgression of one too well known: yet I rather re-joice that you should judge your pleasure over many, than be abused by any.' 'My good *Hope*,' quod he, 'it were not reason that after such manifold promises of your exceeding courte-sies, I should use strange and contentious speech with so dear a friend, and indeed I must confess that the opinion which I have received of my mistress, hath stirred my pen to write very hardly against all the feminine gender, but I pray you pardon me,' quod he, 'and if it please you I will recant: as I also (percase) I was but cloyed with *surquedry*, and pre-sumed to think more than may be proved.' 'Yea but how if it were proved?' quod Dame *Frances*. 'If were so (which God forbid),' quod he, 'then could you not blame me to conceive that opinion.' 'Howsoever I might blame you,' quod she, 'I mean not to blame you, but I demand further, if it be as I think and you suspect, what will you then do?' 'Surely,' quod *F.J.*, 'I have determined to drink up mine own sorrow secretly, and to bid them both adieu.' 'I like your farewell better than your fantasy,' quod she, 'and whensoever you can be content to take so much pains, as the knight (which had a nightgown guarded with naked swords) did take, I think you may put yourself out of doubt of all these things.' By these words and other speech which she uttered unto him, *F.J.* smelt how the world went about, and therefore did one day in the grey morning adventure to pass through the gallery towards his mistress' chamber, hoping to have found the door open, but he found the contrary, and there attending in good devotion, heard the parting of his mistress and her secretary, with many kind words: whereby it appeared that the one was

128

very loth to part with the other. *F.J.* was enforced to bear this burden, and after he had attended there as long as the light would give him leave, he departed also to his chamber, and apparelling himself, could not be quiet until he had spoken with his mistress, whom he burdened flatly with this despiteful treachery: and she as fast denied it, until at last being still urged with such evident tokens as he alleged, she gave him this bone to gnaw upon. 'And if I did so,' quod she, 'what then?' Whereunto *F.J.* made none answer, but departed with this farewell. *'My loss is mine own, and your gain is none of yours, and sooner can I recover my loss than you enjoy the gain which you gape after.'* And when he was in place solitary, he compiled these following for a final end of the matter.

G.T.

And if I did what then?
Are you aggrieved therefore?
The sea hath fish for every man,
And what would you have more?

Thus did my mistress once,
Amaze my mind with doubt;
And popped a question for the nonce,
To beat my brains about.

Whereto I thus replied
Each fisherman can wish,
That all the sea at every tide,
Were his alone to fish.

And so did I (in vain),
But since it may not be:
Let such fish there as find the gain,
And leave the loss for me.

And with such luck and loss,
I will content myself:
Till tides of turning time may toss,
Such fishers on the shelf.

And when they stick on sands,
That every man may see:

Then will I laugh and clap my hands,
As they do now at me.

F.J.

It is time now to make an end of this thriftless history, wherein although I could wade much further, as to declare his departure, what thanks he gave his *Hope*, &c. yet will I cease, as one that had rather leave it unperfect than to make it plain . . .

G.T.

from THE SPOIL OF ANTWERP. Faithfully reported by a
true Englishman, who was present at the same. *(November 1576)*

. . . I was lodged in the English house *ut supra*, and had not
gone abroad that morning by reason of weighty business
which I had in hand the same day. At dinner time the mer-
chantmen of my country which came out of the town, and
dined in my chamber, told me that a hot scarmouch was
begun in the castle yard, and that the fury thereof still in-
creased. About the middest of dinner, news came that the
shot was so thick, as neither ground, houses, nor people
could be discerned for the smoke thereof: and before dinner
were fully ended, that the Spaniards were like to win the
trenches. Whereat I stepped from the table, and went hastily
up into a high tower of the said English house; from whence
I might discover the fire in four or five places of the town,
towards the castle yard. and thereby was I well assured that
the Spaniards indeed were entered within the trenches. So
that I came down and took my cloak and sword, to see the
certainty thereof, and as I passed toward the Bourse, I met
many, but I overtook none: and those which I met were no
townsmen, but soldiers: neither walked they as men which
use traffic, but ran as men which are in fear: whereat being
somewhat grieved, and seeing the townsmen stand every man
before his door with such weapons as they had, I demanded
of one of them, what it meant? Who answered me in these
words, 'Helas, mounsieur, il n'y a point de ordre, & voila la
ruine de ceste ville.' 'Aiez courage mon amy,' quoth I, and so
went onwards yet towards the Bourse, meeting all the way
more and more which mended their pace. At last, a Walloon
trumpeter on horseback (who seemed to be but a boy of
years) drew his sword, and laid about him crying, 'Ou est que
vous eufuiez canaille? Faisons teste pour le honeur de la patrie.'
Wherewith, fifty or three score of them turned head, and
went backwards towards the Bourse. The which encouraged
me (*per companie*) to proceed: but alas, this comfort endured
but a while: for by that time I came on the farder side of the
Bourse, I might see a great troop coming in greater haste,
with their heads as close together, as a shoal of young fry, or
a flock of sheep: who met me on the farder side of the
Bourse, toward the market place: and having their leaders

foremost (for I knew them by the javelins, boarspears, and staves) bare me over backwards, and ran over my belly and my face, long time before I could recover on foot. At last when I was up, I looked on every side, and seeing them run so fast, began thus to bethink me. What in God's name do I here which have no interest in this action? since they who came to defend this town are content to leave it at large, and shift for themselves: and whilst I stood thus musing, another flock of fliers came so fast that they bare me on my nose, and ran as many over my back, as erst had marched over my guts. In fine, I got up like a tall fellow, and went with them for company; but their haste was such, as I could never over-take them, until I came at a broad cross street which lieth between the English house and the said Bourse: there I over-took some of them grovelling on the ground, and groaning for the last gasp, and some other which turned backwards to avoid the tickling of the Spanish muskets: who had gotten the ends of the said broad cross street, and flanked it both ways: and there I stayed a while till hearing the shot increase, and fearing to be surprised with such as might follow in tail of us, I gave adventure to pass through the said cross street, and (without vaunt be it spoken) passed through five hun-dred shot, before I could recover the English house.

At my coming thither, I found many of the merchants standing before the gate: whom I would not discomfort nor dismay, but said that the Spaniards had once entered the town, and that I hoped they were gone back again: never-theless I went to the Governor, and privily persuaded him to draw in the company and shut up the gates: the which he consented unto, and desired me because I was somewhat better acquainted with such matters than the merchants, to take charge of the key: I took it willingly, but before I could well shut and bar the gates, the Spaniards were now come forwards into the same street: and passing by the door, called to come in: bestowing five or six musket shot at the grate where I answered them, whereof one came very near my nose, and piercing through the gate, struck one of the mer-chants on the head, without any great or dangerous hurt: but the heat of the pursuit was yet such, that they could not attend the spoil, but passed on in chase to the new town, where they slew infinite numbers of people: and by three of the clock,

132

or before returned victors, having slain or put to flight all their enemies. And now to keep promise, and to speak without partiality: I must needs confess, that it was the greatest victory, and the roundliest executed, that hath been seen, read, or heard of, in our age: and that it was a thing miraculous, to consider, how trenches of such a height should entered, passed over, and won both by footmen, and horsemen: for immediately after that the footmen were gotten in, the horsemen found means to follow: and being of them many arquebusiers on horseback, did pass by their own footmen in the streets, and much hastened both the flight of the Walloons, and made the way opener unto speedy execution.

But whosoever will therein most extol the Spaniards for their valour and order, must therewithal confess that it was the very ordinance of God for a just plague and scourge unto the town: for otherwise it passeth all men's capacity, to conceive how it may be possible. And yet the disorder and lack of foresight in the Walloons did great help to augment the Spanish glory and boast. To conclude, the County *de Everstine* was drowned in the new town: the Marquise *de Haurey* and *Champaigne* escaped out of the said new town, and recovered the Prince of Orange's ships: only the young Count *de Egmont* was taken fighting by St. Michael's. *M. de Capres* & *M. de Goonie* were also taken: but I heard of none that fought stoutly, only the said Count *de Egmont*, whom the *Colonel Verdugo*, a Spaniard of an honourable compassion and good mind, did save with great danger to himself in defending the Count. In this conflict were there slain six hundred Spaniards or thereabouts: and on the Thursday next following, a view of the dead bodies in the town being taken, it was esteemed at 17,000 men, women, and children. A pitiful massacre though God gave victory to the Spaniards. And surely, as their dalliance was to be much commended, so yet I can much discommend their barbarous cruelty, in many respects: for methinks, that as when God giveth abundance of wealth, the owner ought yet to have regard on whom he bestow it: even so, when God giveth a great and miraculous victory, the conquerors ought to have great regard unto their execution: and though some, which favour the Spanish faction, will allege sundry reasons to the contrary, yet when the blood is cold, and the fury over, methinks that a true

Christian heart should stand content with victory, and refrain to provoke God's wrath by shedding of innocent blood. These things I rehearse (the rather) because they neither spared age, nor sex: profession nor religion: young nor old: rich nor poor: strong nor feeble: but without any mercy, did tyrannously triumph when there was neither man nor mean to resist them: for age and sex, young and old, they slew great numbers of young children, but many more women more than fourscore years of age: for time and place, their fury was as great ten days after the victory, as at the time of their entry: and as great respect they had to the church and churchyard, (for all their hypocritical boasting of the Catholic religion) as the butcher hath to his shambles or slaughterhouse: for person and country they spared neither friend nor foe: Portingal nor Turk: for profession and religion, the Jesuits must give their ready coin: and all other religious houses both coin and plate with all short ends that were good and portable. The rich was spoiled because he had: and the poor were hanged because they had nothing: neither strength could prevail to make resistance, nor weakness move pity to refrain their horrible cruelty. And this was not only done when the chase was hot, but (as I erst said) when the blood was cold, and they now victors without resistance. I refrain to rehearse the heaps of dead carcasses which lay at every trench where they entered: the thickness whereof, did in many places exceed the height of a man.

I forbear also to recount the huge numbers, drowned in the new town: where a man might behold as many sundry shapes and forms of man's motion at time of death: as ever *Michaelangelo* did portray in his tables of Doomsday. I list not to reckon the infinite numbers of poor Almains, who lay burned in their armour: from the entrails scorched out, and all the rest of the body free, some their heads and shoulders burnt off: so that you might look down into the bulk and breast and there take an anatomy of the secrets of nature. Some standing upon their waist, being burnt off by the thighs: and some no more than the very top of the brain taken off with fire, whiles the rest of the body did abide unspeakable torments. I set not down the ugly and filthy polluting of every street with the gore and carcasses of men and horses: neither do I complain, that the one lacked burial, and the

134

other flaying, until the air (corrupted with their carrion) infected all that remained alive in the town: and why should I describe the particularity of every such annoyance, as commonly happen both in camps and castles, where martial feats are managed? But I may not pass over with silence, the wilful burning and destroying of the Townhouse, and all the monuments and records of the city: neither can I refrain to tell their shameful rapes and outrageous forces presented unto sundry honest dames and virgins. It is a thing too horrible to rehearse, that the father and mother were forced to fetch their young daughter out of a cloister (who had thither fled as unto sanctuary, to keep her body undefiled) and to bestow her in bed between two Spaniards, to work their wicked and detestable will with her.

It is also a ruthful remembrance, that a poor English merchant (who was but a servant) having once redeemed his master's goods for three hundred crowns, was yet hanged until he were half dead, because he had not two hundred more to give them: and the halter being cut down, and he commen to himself again, besought them to give him leave to seek and try his credit and friends in the town, for the rest of their unreasonable demand. At his return because he sped not (as indeed no money was to be had) they hung him again outright: and afterwards (of exceeding courtesy) procured the Friars *minor* to bury him.

To conclude, of the seventeen thousand carcasses, which were viewed on the Thursday, I think in conscience, that five thousand or few less, were massacred after their victory, because they had not ready money, wherewith to ransom their goods at such prices as they pleased to see on them: at least all the world will bear me witness, that ten (yea twenty days) after, whosoever were but pointed at, and named to be a Walloon, was immediately massacred without furder audience or trial. For mine own part, it is well known that I did often escape very narrowly, because I was taken for a Walloon. And on Sunday, the eleventh of this instant (which was the day before I got out of the town) I saw three poor souls murdered in my presence, because they were pointed to be Walloons: and it was well proved immediately that one of them was a poor artificer, who had dwelt in the town eight years before, and never managed arms, but truly followed his occupation:

135

furthermore the seed of these and other barbarous facts brought forth this crop and fruit: that within three days *Antwerp*, which was one of the richest towns in Europe, had now no money nor treasure to be found therein, but only in the hands of murderers and strumpets: for every *Dom Diego* must walk jetting up and down the streets with his harlot by him in her chain and bracelets of gold. And the notable Bourse which was wont to be a safe assembly for merchants, and men of all honest trades, had now none other merchandise therein, but as many dicing tables as might be placed round about it all day long.

Men will boast of the Spaniards that they are the best and most orderly soldiers in the world: but sure, if this be their order, I had rather be counted a *besoigner*, than a brave soldier in such a band: neither must we think (although it hath pleased God for some secret cause only known to his divine Majesty, to yield Antwerp and Maestrecht, thus into their hands) that he will spare to punish this their outrageous cruelty, when his good will and pleasure shall be to do the same: for surely their boasting and bragging of iniquity, is over great to escape long unscourged . . .

'CERTAIN NOTES OF INSTRUCTION CONCERNING THE MAKING OF VERSE OR RHYME IN ENGLISH WRITTEN AT THE REQUEST OF MASTER EDOUARDO DONATI'
(*from* Posies, *1575*)

Signor Edouardo, since promise is debt, and you (by the law of friendship) do burden me with a promise that I should lend you instructions towards the making of English verse or rhyme, I will essay to discharge the same, though not so perfectly as I would, yet as readily as I may: and therewithal I pray you consider that *quot homines, tot sententiae*, especially in poetry, wherein (nevertheless) I dare not challenge any degree, and yet will I at your request adventure to set down my simple skill in such simple manner as I have used, referring the same hereafter to the correction of the *Laureate*. And you shall have it in these few points following.

The first and most necessary point that ever I found meet to be considered in making of a delectable poem is this, to ground it upon some fine invention. For it is not enough to roll in pleasant words, nor yet to thunder in *Rym, Ram, Ruff*, by letter (quoth my master *Chaucer*) nor yet to abound in apt vocables, or epithets, unless the invention have in it *aliquid salis*, I mean some *good and fine invention*, I mean that I would have it both fine and good. For many inventions are so superfine, that they are *vix* good. And again many inventions are *good*, and yet not *finely* handled. And for the general forewarning: what theme soever you do take in hand, if you handle it but *tanquam in oratione perpetua*, and never study for some depth of device in the invention, and some figures also in the handling thereof: it will appear to the skilful reader but a tale of a tub. To deliver unto you general examples it were almost unpossible, sithence the occasions of inventions are (as it were) infinite: nevertheless take in worth mine opinion, and perceive my further meaning in these few points. If I should undertake to write in praise of a gentlewoman, I would neither praise her crystal eye, nor her cherry lip, etc. For these things are *trita & obvia*. But I would either find some supernatural cause whereby my pen might walk in the superlative degree, or else I would undertake to answer for any imperfection that she hath, and thereupon raise the praise of her commendation. Likewise if I should disclose my pretence in love, I would either make a strange discourse of some intolerable passion, or find occasion to plead by the example of some history, or discover my disquiet in shadows *per allegoriam*, or use the covertest mean that I could to avoid the uncomely customs of common writers. Thus much I adventure to deliver unto you (my friend) upon the rule of invention, which of all other rules is most to be marked, and hardest to be prescribed in certain and infallible rules, nevertheless to conclude therein, I would have you stand most upon the excellency of your invention, and stick not to study deeply for some fine device. For that being found, pleasant words will follow well enough and fast enough.

2 Your invention being once devised, take heed that neither pleasure of rhyme, nor variety of device, do carry you far from it: for us to use obscure and dark phrases in a pleasant sonnet, is nothing delectable, so to intermingle merry jests in a serious matter is an *indecorum*.

3 I will next advise you that you hold the just measure wherewith you begin your verse, I will not deny but this may seem a preposterous order: but because I covet rather to satisfy you particularly, than to undertake a general tradition, I will not so much stand upon the manner as the matter of my precepts. I say then, remember to hold the same measure wherewith you begin, whether it be in a verse of six syllables, eight, ten, twelve, etc. and though this precept may seem ridiculous unto you, since every young scholar can conceive that he ought to continue in the same measure wherewith he beginneth, yet do I see and read many men's poems nowadays, which beginning with the measure of xii in the first line, and xiv in the second (which is the common kind of verse) they will yet (by that time they have passed over a few verses) fall into xiv and fourteen, & *sic de similibus*, the which is either forgetfulness or carelessness.

4 And in your verses remember to place every word in his natural *emphasis* or sound, that is to say in such wise, and with such length or shortness, elevation or depression of syllables, as it is commonly pronounced or used: to express the same we have three manner of accents, *gravis*, *levis*, & *circumflexa*, the which I would English thus, the long accent,

the short accent, and that which is indifferent: the grave accent is marked by this character, /, the light accent is noted thus, , & the circumflex or indifferent is thus signified   : the grave accent is drawn out or elevate, and maketh that syllable long whereupon it is placed: the light accent is depressed or snatched up, and maketh that syllable short upon which it lighteth: the circumflex accent is indifferent, sometimes short, sometimes long, sometimes depressed and sometimes elevate. For example of the emphasis or natural sound of words, this word *treasure*, hath the grave accent upon the first syllable, whereas if it should be written in this sort, *treasure*, now were the second syllable long, and that were clean contrary to the common use, wherewith it is pronounced. For further explanation hereof, note you that commonly nowadays in English rhymes (for I dare not call them English verses) we use none other but a foot of two syllables, whereof the first is depressed or made short, and the second is elevate or made long: and that sound or scanning continueth throughout the verse. We have used in time past other kinds of metres: as for example this following:

No wight in this world, that wealth can attain

Unless he believe, that all is but vain.

Also our father *Chaucer* hath used the same liberty in feet and measures that the Latinists do use: and whosoever do peruse and well consider his words, he shall find that although his lines are not always of one selfsame number of syllables, yet being read by one that hath understanding, the longest verse and that which hath most syllables in it, will fall (to the ear) correspondent unto that which hath fewest syllables in it: and likewise that which hath in it fewest syllables, shall be found yet to consist of words that have such natural sound, as may seem equal in length to a verse which hath many more syllables of lighter accents. And surely I can lament that we are fallen into such a plain and simple manner of writing, that there is none other foot used but one: whereby our poems may justly be called rhythms, and cannot by any right challenge the name of a verse. But since it is so, let us take the ford as we find it, and let me set down unto you such rules or precepts that even in this plain foot of two syllables you wrest no word from his natural and usual sound, I do not mean that you may use none other words but of two syllables, for therein you may use discretion according to occasion of matter: but my meaning is, that all the words in your verse be so placed as the first syllable may sound short or depressed, the second long or elevate, the third short, the fourth long, the fifth short, etc. For example of my meaning in this point mark these two verses:

I understand your meaning by your eye.

Your meaning I understand by your eye.

In these two verses there seemeth no difference at all since the one hath the very self same words that the other hath, and yet the latter verse is neither true nor pleasant, & the first verse may pass the musters. The fault of the latter verse is that this word *understand* is therein so placed as the grave accent falleth on *der*, and thereby maketh *der*, in this word understand to be elevated: which is contrary to the natural or usual pronunciation: for we say

understand, and not

understand.

5 Here by the way I think it not amiss to forewarn you that you thrust as few words of many syllables into your verse as may be: and hereunto I might allege many reasons: first the most ancient English words are of one syllable, so that the more monosyllables you use, the truer Englishman you shall seem and the less you shall smell of the inkhorn. Also words of many syllables do cloy a verse and make it unpleasant, whereas words of one syllable will more easily fall to be short or long as occasion requireth, or will be adapted to become circumflex or of an indifferent sound.

6 I would exhort you also to beware of rhyme without reason: my meaning is hereby that your rhyme lead you not

from your first invention, for so many writers when they have laid the platform of their invention, are yet drawn sometimes (by rhyme) to forget it or at least to alter it, as when they cannot readily find out a word which may rhyme to the first (and yet continue the determinate invention) they do then either botch it up with a word that will rhyme (how small reason soever it carry with it) or else they alter their first word and so percase decline or trouble their former invention: but do you always hold your first determined invention, and do rather search the bottom of your brains for apt words, than change good reason for rumbling rhyme.

7 To help you a little with rhyme (which is also a plain young scholar's lesson) work thus, when you have set down your first verse, take the last word thereof and count over all the words of the self same sound by order of the alphabet: as for example, the last word of your first line is *care*, to rhyme therewith you have *bare, clare, dare, fare, gare, hare, and share, mare, snare, rare, stare, and ware, etc.* Of all these take that which best may serve your purpose, carrying reason with rhyme: and if none of them will serve so, then alter the last word of your former verse, but yet do not willingly alter the meaning of your invention.

8 You may use the same figures or tropes in verse which are used in prose, and in my judgement they serve more aptly, and have greater grace in verse than they have in prose: but yet therein remember the old adage, *ne quid nimis*, as many writers which do not know the use of any other figure than that which is expressed in repetition of sundry words beginning all with one letter, the which (being modestly used) lendeth good grace to a verse: but they do so hunt a letter to death, that they make it *crambé*, and *crambe bis positum mors est*: therefore *ne quid nimis*.

9 Also as much as may be, eschew strange words, or *obsoleta & inusitata*, unless the theme do give just occasion: marry in some places a strange word doth draw attentive reading, but yet I would have you therein to use discretion.

10 And as much as you may, frame your style to *perspicuity* and to be sensible: for the haughty obscure verse doth not much delight, and the verse that is too easy is like the tale of a roasted horse: but let your poem be such as may

both delight and draw attentive reading, and therewithal may deliver such matter as be worth the marking.

11 You shall do very well to use your verse after the English phrase, and not after the manner of other languages: the Latinists do commonly set the adjective after the substantive: as for example *femina pulchra, aedes altae, etc.* but if we should say in English a woman fair, a house high, etc., it would have but small grace: for we say a good man, and not a man good, etc. And yet I will not altogether forbid it you, for in some places, it may be born, but not so hardly as some use it which write thus:

> Now let us go to temple ours,
> I will go visit mother mine, etc.

Surely I smile at the simplicity of such devisers which might as well have said it in plain English phrase, and yet have better pleased all ears, than satisfy their own fancies by such *superfinesse*. Therefore even as I have advised you to place all words in their natural or most common and usual pronunciation, so would I wish you to frame all sentences in their mother phrase and proper *idiom*, and yet sometimes (as I have said before) the contrary may be born, but that is rather where rhyme enforceth, or *per licentiam poeticam*, than it is otherwise lawful or commendable.

12 This poetical licence is a shrewd fellow, and causeth many faults in a verse, it maketh words longer, shorter, of more syllables, of fewer, newer, older, truer, falser, and to conclude it turkeneth all things at pleasure, for example *ydone* for *done, adown* for *down, orecome* for *overcome, tane* for *taken, power* for *powre, heaven* for *heavn, thewes* for good parts or good qualities, and a number of other which were but tedious and needless to rehearse, since your own judgement and reading will soon make you espy such advantages.

13 There are also certain pauses or rests in a verse which may be called *ceasures*, whereof I would be loth to stand long, since it is at discretion of the writer, and they have been first devised (as should seem) by the musicians: but yet thus much I will adventure to write, that in mine opinion in a verse of eight syllables, the pause will stand best in the middest, in a verse of ten it will best be placed at the end of the first

four syllables: in a verse of twelve, in the first and fourteen in the second, we place the pause commonly in the midst of the first, and at the end of the first eight syllables in the second. In Rhythm Royal, it is at the writer's discretion, and forceth not where the pause be until the end of the line.

14 And here because I have named Rhythm Royal, I will tell you also mine opinion as well of that as of the names which other rhymes have commonly born heretofore. Rhythm Royal is a verse of ten syllables, and seven such verses make a staff, whereof the first and third lines do answer (across) in like terminations and rhyme, the second, fourth, and fifth, do likewise answer each other in terminations, and the last two do combine and shut up the sentence: this hath been called Rhythm Royal, and surely it is a royal kind of verse, serving best for grave discourse. There is also another kind called ballade, and thereof are sundry sorts: for a man may write ballade in a staff of six lines, every line containing eight or six syllables, whereof the first and third, second and fourth do rhyme together in conclusion. You may write also your ballade of ten syllables rhyming as before is declared, but these two were wont to be most commonly used in ballade, which proper name was (I think) derived from this word in Italian *ballare*, which signifieth to dance. And indeed those kinds of rhyme serve best for dances or light matters. Then have you also a rondelet, the which doth always end with one selfsame foot or repetition, and was therefore (in my judgement) called a rondelet. This may consist of such measure as best liketh the writer, then have you sonnets, some think that all poems (being short) may be called sonnets, as indeed it is a diminutive word derived of *sonare*, but yet I can best allow to call those sonnets which are of fourteen lines, every line containing ten syllables. The first twelve do rhyme in staves of four lines by cross metre, and the last two rhyming together do conclude the whole. There are dizaines, and sixaines which are of ten lines, and five lines, which some English writers do also term by the name of sonnets. Then there is an old kind of rhythm called verlays, derived (as I have read) of this word *verd* which signifieth green, and *lay* which betokeneth a song, as if you could say green songs: but I must tell you by the way, that I never read any verse which I saw by authority called *verlay*,

but one, and that was a long discourse in verses of ten syllables, whereof the four first did rhyme across, and the fifth did answer to the first and third, breaking off there, and so going on to another termination. Of this I could show example of imitation in mine own verses written to the Right Honourable Lord *Grey* of *Wilton* upon my journey to *Holland*, etc. There are also certain poems devised of ten syllables, whereof the first answereth in termination with the fourth, and the second and third answer each other: these are more used by other nations than by us, neither can I tell readily what name to give them. And the commonest sort of verse which we use nowadays (*viz.* the long verse of twelve and fourteen syllables) I know not certainly how to name it, unless I should say that it doth consist of poulters' measure, which giveth xii for one dozen and xiiii for another. But let this suffice (if it be not too much) for the sundry sorts of verses which we use nowadays.

15 In all these sorts of verses whensoever you undertake to write, avoid prolixity and tediousness, and ever as near as you can, do finish the sentence and meaning at the end of every staff where you write staves, and at the end of every two lines where you write by couples or poulters' measure: for I see many writers which draw their sentence in length, and make an end at latter Lammas: for commonly before they end, the reader hath forgotten where he begun. But do you (if you will follow my advice) eschew prolixity and knit up your sentences as compendiously as you may, since brevity (so that it be not drowned in obscurity) is most commendable.

16 I had forgotten a notable kind of rhyme, called riding rhyme, and that is such as your master and father *Chaucer* used in his Canterbury Tales, and in divers other delectable and light enterprises: but though it come to my remembrance somewhat out of order, it shall not come altogether out of time, for I will now tell you a conceit which I had before forgotten to write: you may see (by the way) that I hold a preposterous order in my traditions, but as I said before I write moved by good will, and not to show my skill. Then to return to my matter, as this riding rhyme serveth most aptly to write a merry tale, so rhythm royal is fittest for a grave discourse. Ballades are best of matters of love, and rondelets

144

most apt for the beating or handling of an adage or common proverb: sonnets serve as well in matters of love as of discourse: dixaines and sixaines for short fantasies: verlays for an effectual proposition, although by the name you might otherwise judge of verlays, and the long verse of twelve and fourteen syllables, although it be nowadays used in all themes, yet in my judgement it would serve best for psalms and hymns.

I would stand longer in these traditions, were it not that I doubt mine own ignorance, but as I said before, I know that I write to my friend, and affixing myself thereupon, I make an end.

EXPLANATORY NOTES

Gascoigne's Posies

These form an identifiable sequence in *A Hundreth Sundry Flowres*, disrupted by the rearrangement into *The Posies*, and replaced by one in later works.

Si fortunatus infoelix — if successful, yet unhappy
Spraeta tamen vivunt — let them live in spite of disdain
Ferenda Natura — Nature bearing the blame
Meritum petere, grave — To seek due reward is responsible (parodied by Harvey as *meritum petere, vile*).
Ever or Never
Haud ictus sapio — unwise, despite troubles
Attamen ad solitum — nevertheless, as usual (used once only)
Sic tuli — thus I bore (my burden)
Fato non fortuna — by fate, not by fortune

Tam Marti, quam Mercurio — literally, as much to Mars as to Mercury; so, a soldier-poet. Gascoigne's personal posy from 1576.

Explanatory Notes

p. 25 'This vain avail . . .'
  Intro. 'courses at the ring' — a tilting contest
  2. 'field' — i.e., of war
  8. 'reave' — plunder
  16. 'earst' — at first
  22. 'tear a golden time' — to waste time in some Arcadia
  26. 'Pan' here signifies natural, 'Pallas' intellectual knowledge.
  30. 'Shadows' may refer to book-learning; but, more likely, 'when shadows make thee sure' may mean 'when you are deceived'.

p. 26 'Of all the birds . . .'
  Sparrows were thought to be particularly lecherous in this period.
  9. 'list' — wants
  23. 'fend cut' — a defensive manoeuvre in fencing
  24. 'peat' — term of endearment for a girl

p. 28 'Thy birth, thy beauty . . .'
  16. 'in mew' — restrained
  29. 'fere' — companion
  47. 'my stomach will I starve' — I will restrain my anger

p. 29 'That self same tongue . . .'
   9. 'hardily' — boldly

p. 30 'Of all the letters . . .'
   Much of the poem plays on the initials of Gascoigne's own name, those of his wife, Elizabeth Bacon Breton, and her supposed husband, Edward Boyes. (This is one of the few poems to be omitted altogether from the *Posies*.)
   1. 'Christ's cross row' — alphabet
   9. 'behove' — benefit, advantage
   27. 'sol, re, ut' — notes on the scale, together they form a chord.
   31. 'percase' — perhaps
   39. 'wight' — man

p. 31 'A lady once . . .'
   3. 'quod' — said
   The answer is a kiss.

p. 31 'At Beauty's bar . . .'
   14. 'it sitteth not' — it is unfitting
   16. 'wote' — know
   19. 'quest' — inquest
   20. 'fere' — partner
   21. 'pickthanks' — tell-tales
   24. 'trussed' — hung

p. 33 'Sing lullaby . . .'
   16. 'beguile' — divert (from the painful fact that this applies to you)
   24. 'eft' — again
   34. Gascoigne's son was not called Robin; it probably means the phallus.

p. 35 'If yielding fear . . .'
   Intro. 'audaces fortuna iuvat' — fortune favours the brave.
   11. Ascanius was the son of Aeneas and founder of Alba Longa.

p. 35 'The vain excess . . .'
   Intro. 'satis sufficit' — enough is adequate
   16. 'eke' — as well
   19. 'leek' — proverbially of little value
   26. 'shent' — disgraceful
   38. 'foiled' — violated (of chastity)
   39. 'prick'st thou many a pin' — probably obscene; roughly, 'you will go fornicating elsewhere'.

p. 37 'The common speech . . .'
　　Intro. 'magnum vectiglia parcimonia' — thrift makes a good income.
　　2. 'a bottle . . . etc.' — the equipment of a vagrant
　　6-7. start economising when your account is full; that will save you
from spending the last of it.
　　8. 'list' — likes to
　　12. 'clouts' — patches
　　13. 'goonhole groats' — low value coins
　　14. 'crowns' — higher value coins
　　16. the man who spends a lot on hats
　　23. 'angels' — another coin
　　25. 'haggard' — wild, untrained
　　27. 'mercer' — draper
　　35. 'cates' — delicacies
　　36. 'stound' — wooden vessel
　　39. 'tenterhooks' — crooked nails with sharp ends
　　42. 'hooches' — cheats

p. 38 'In haste post haste . . .'
　　The first sonnet sequence in English, along with the *terza sequenza*
in *Master F.J.*.
　　Intro. 'Sat cito, si sat bene' — let it be done quickly if it's good.
　　'Nimis cito' — too much haste
　　'Vix bene' — hardly well
　　25. 'wanhope' — despair
　　35. 'bravery' — display (esp. fine clothes)
　　42. 'prink up' — dress up ostentatiously
　　79. 'tickle' — changeable, fickle

p. 41 'When peerless Princes' courts . . .'
　　Intro. 'Durum aeneum & miserabile aevum' — a hard, brazen, pitiless
age. (Brazen as opposed to the gold & silver ages.)
　　2. 'quest' — those bringing an action
　　13. 'Lycurgus' — a Spartan lawgiver whose brother was King. His wife
proposed to Lycurgus that she would kill her children if he'd share the
throne with her. At the birth of the posthumous son, Lycurgus pro-
claimed him King and left Sparta.
　　34. 'Clim of the Clough' — a rustic from the ballads
All the characters in 25-40 are typical of mystery plays and interludes
still being performed in Gascoigne's time.
　　36. 'gear' — affair, 'goings on'
　　39. 'counter' — also the name for the debtors' prison
　　42. 'fret' — wear away
　　46. 'crosier' — a bishop's staff or crook (& thus a play on 'crooked')

149

p. 43 'My reckless race . . .'
   Title. 'Dominus iis opus habet'—the Lord hath need of them (Mat.21.3)
     10. 'pelf' — riches (derogatory)
     17. 'gis' — abbreviation of 'Jesus' for exclamations
     21. 'roast' — always thus in sixteenth-century versions of this phrase
     27. 'meed' — mercy
     40. 'durante bene placido' — it lasts as long as I please
           'jade' — decrepit horse
     66. 'neat' — cattle
     78. 'cates' — provisions, fancies
     91. 'lubber' — servant, drudge
     94. 'Hallontide' — All Hallows, 1 November
     104. 'mesne land' (pronounced 'main') — (feudal) land held by an inferior lord from a superior
     105. 'pelters prate' — inferiors talk

p. 46 'You that have spent . . .'
     15. 'sprite' — spirit
     53. 'Phoebus' — the sun

p. 49 'Mine own . . .'
Bartholomew Withipoll was a friend Gascoigne may have met at Cambridge.
     14. 'geazon' — rare
     23. 'Prime' and 'Hour' — monastic prayer services
     24. 'Nostre Dieu' — our God
     67. 'fay' — faith
     73. 'fico' — fig
     76. 'spell' — also means 'relieve yourself'
     78, 82. Spaniards were reputedly notorious poisoners
     88. 'bumbast' — stuffing
     96. 'for the nonce' — on purpose (but often in poetry of this period as a meaningless filler)
     109. 'coptankt' — high-crowned
     111. pantaloons tight over the waist and buttocks
     112. 'curtold slipper' — with a curled point
     121ff. In the *Posies* the pox is substituted for papistry, possibly to avoid offending Gascoigne's Catholic friends and patrons the Montagues.
     127. 'polshorn' — tonsured
     132. Catholicism and atheism were often twinned accusations in Reformation England.
     144. 'feres' — friends
     146-7. Withipoll's travelling companions
     150. Spa is near Liege in modern Belgium, and thus just reachable by Gascoigne while campaigning in the Netherlands.
     154. 'in gree' — in good part

p. 54 'My worthy Lord . . .'
Intro. 'cum pertinenciis' — with all that relates to it
3. 'amazed' — a stronger word than now; the sense of being stuck in a maze closer to the surface.
5. 'carrion' — with young and therefore unfit to eat
19. 'make avow' — explain
22. Littleton's *Tenures* was a standard textbook for law students. 'Undoubtedly the most crabbed author to begin with of any science in the world.' (John Cooke, a seventeenth-century lawyer)
23. 'daw' — simpleton
24. Sir Antony Fitzherbert's *La Grande Abridgement* was the first attempt to systematise English law.
26. 'Tully' — Cicero, a model for style at this time
34. 'wield' — control
50. 'gay' — ornament
58. 'bit' — mouth
75. 'sakeless' — innocent
81. 'pill' — pillage
105. Parkins, Rastell and Bracton were all legal authors
148. 'the whites' — the centre of the target

p. 58 'If any flower . . .'
'Quoniam . . .' — Even to those of low station, pleasant places are delightful.

p. 59. 'A strange conceit . . .'
1. 'conceit' — idea (cf. 'invention' in *Certain Notes* . . .)
5. 'alderlievest' — 'best beloved' (*Posies* margin)
10. 'pastaunce' — pastime
12. 'en bon gré' — 'in good work' (*Posies* margin)
17. 'leas' — fields
20. 'welkin' — sky
25. 'galled' — vex
42. 'ferly' —strange
62. 'aloof' — turn the ship to windward
66. 'hull' — 'when all sails are taken down' (*Posies* margin)
69. 'butterbitten' — fat from eating butter
70. 'swad' — clodhopper
71. 'tone' — taken
72. 'Ghy zijt te vroegh' — 'You be too soon' (*Posies* margin)
73. 'Tis niet goet tijt' — 'It is not good tide' (*Posies* margin)
76. 'Alba's' — The Duke of Alva was the Spanish commander in the Netherlands.
89. Pun on Pontius Pilate (cf. 272)
91. 'small smack' — little idea

92. Gascoigne plays on the traditional association of the Dutch and drink to suggest their language inebriates.

101. 'Dansk' — modern Gdansk, or Danzig

102. 'Frize' — Friesland

107. 'uncouth' — unknown

111. 'soun' — sound, the area of sea

120. 'It is good tide that know I well'(*Posies* margin)

125. 'bale' — suffering

127. Psalm 107 is about the Lord rescuing people in their distress.

132 'Edel Bloetts' — 'Lusty gallants' (*Posies* margin)

139. 'fleet and flow' — drift with the current

150. 'blin' — fail

189. 'bane' — destruction

203. The companions were Yorke and Herle (*Posies* margin): Yorke was a London roisterer who later betrayed the town of Zutphen, Herle was one of Walsingham's agents.

205. 'yfere' — together

207. 'bouge' — suffer a fracture in the bilge

228. 'everychone' — everyone

231. 'Hoy' — small, sloop-rigged vessel

238. 'carke' — 'care' (*Posies* margin)

277. 'trulls' — whores

280. 'in clink' — locked up

284. 'pynke' — 'a small boat' (*Posies* margin)

296. 'buttered beer' — a drink of butter, beer, sugar and spices

297. 'browess' — broth

301. Harlem was besieged from December 1572 to July 1573, and then surrendered to false promises of clemency.

311. 'broad before' — obvious; 'enure' — bring into operation

322. 'yfeare' — together

336. 'met v: and anders niet' — with you and no one else

344-5. Zouche and Denny may have been associates of Grey with an interest in the Irish campaigns. 'mought' — might

347 'smugskinned' — smooth-skinned

349. Moyle was a heretic hunter in Henry VII's time who lived in Kent. 'Behight' — promised

356. 'carts' — charts

p. 68. *Dan Bartholomew*, from 'The Reporter'

61. 'eyne' —old plural of eyes

68. 'flinging' — fatal

69. 'Cressid' — Cressida, a fickle lover. Gascoigne may well have read Chaucer's *Troilus and Criseyde*.

75. 'bedaft' — spoiled

78. 'mell' — honey

93. 'Ferenda Natura' — see *Posies*, 'Nature bearing the blame'

p. 70 'Dan Bartholomew's Dolorous Discourses'
  17. 'whilom' — at that time
  71. 'waymenting' — lamenting
  122. 'Diomede' — Diomedes was Troilus's successor as Cressida's lover
  123. 'wot' — knows
  143. 'hang the lip' — look vexed
  144. 'flocks' — feathers or tufts of material used as stuffing
  180. 'wight' — person
  183. 'scamble in scathe' — make my way as best I can, though hurt
  199. 'When Titan . . .' — i.e., the sunrise
  217. 'fere' — friend
  228. 'brawnfallen' — wasted
  230. 'wearish' — ineffectual
  234. 'bumbast' — stuffing
  241. 'galded' — sore
  242. 'fazed' — unravelled
  248. 'long home' — death (Ecclesiastes)
  254. 'wanhope' — despair
  256. second 'ghost' — spirit, soul
  280. 'surquedry' — pride
  292. 'Ippocrace' — drink of wine, sugar and spices (with pun on 'hypocrisy' to come)
  323. 'prime' — the first hour of the day, usually 6 am.
  337. 'dole' — dolour, misery
  368. 'riding rhyme' — alluded to at the end of *Certain Notes* . . .

p. 80 'Gascoigne's De Profundis'
'De profundis' — out of the depths. (The opening words of Psalm 130, of which the poem is a much extended imitation.) The introduction, but, oddly, not the psalm, is printed in *Flowres*.
  8. 'in gree' — recompense, settlement
  18. 'in ure' — into practice
  33. 'have list to' — decide to

p. 83 'Fancy (quoth he) farewell . . .'
Gascoigne was nicknamed 'the green knight' in the Netherlands, perhaps alluding to his simplicity or inexperience. This poem is part of a short sequence, 'The fruit of fetters', probably written during his imprisonment there.
  11. 'bear the bell' — take first place
  21. 'eke' — also
  22. 'kine' — cows
  24. 'swains' — labourers

32. 'wray' — tell

34. 'raff and ruff' — Chaucerian terms for alliterative verse, as in *Certain Notes* below.

37. 'eft' — once

37, 39. 'sacred sound', 'hierarchies' — in this period the heavens were thought to be arranged according to harmonic proportion.

40. 'monochords' — ancient stringed instrument used to demonstrate mathematical relationships of musical intervals; 'modes' — (1) measuring of a melody, subdividing 'longs' into breves, etc. (2) arrangement of intervals within the scale; 'burdens' — drone or bass part

45. 'proyne' — prune

47. 'griff' — graft

p. 85 'Soldiers behold . . .'

stanza 150 'powdering tub' — barrel in which meat was salted or pickled.

154. 'ell' — a measurement: the English ell was 45'', the Flemish 27''

191. 'saunder stuff' — private anger

p. 89 'Are minds of men . . .'

3. 'silly' — defenceless, pitiful (standard poetic epithet for animals)

12. 'wrack for ruth' — persecution instead of pity

14. 'blaze' — proclaim

39. 'endue' — digest

p. 90 'But that my Lord . . .'

44. 'my Lord' — the poem is addressed to Lord Grey of Wilton

45. 'mysteries' — significance

65. seditious speech was punished by nailing both ears to the pillory, or cutting them off.

72. 'flearing' — smiling, fawning

75. 'Sym Swash' — a swashbuckler; 'buckler' — small round shield, used as a symbol of office

84. 'make' — mate

85. 'percase' — perhaps

112. 'fact' — deed

116. 'compeer' — fellow

128. 'wray' — expose

181. 'berral glass' — a mirror whose reflective power came from staining the glass brown.

185. 'foil' — metal backing of glass mirror

p. 93. 'aliquid salis' — something of value
'frowardness' — perversity, contrary nature
'fire in frost' — the state of the lover's feelings as described by Petrarch, as well as passion in the north.
'besprent' — sprinkled
'brake the brawl' — left the ring of dancers

p. 94. 'humours' — the balance of the humours, the various liquids in the body, was believed to determine the psychological balance of the subject, whose face (red, dark, pale, etc.) would show which humour was in the ascendancy.

p. 95. 'bewrayeth' — shows

p. 97. 'camnassado' — surprise attack by night

p. 98. 'congé' — farewell
'bezo las manos' — kiss the hands
'zuccado des labros' — kiss on the lips
'percase' — perhaps

p. 99. 'galded' — made sore
'devoir' — duty

p. 100. 'conceits' — ideas
'rounding' — whispering
'orisons' — prayers

p. 101. 'made semblant to mistrust' — pretended to be afraid. (The recitation of multiple prayers, usually in Latin, was widely thought to have curative powers; as were hazel twigs)

p. 102. 'your hand on your halfpenny' — have a particular end in view

p. 103. 'cocklorel's music' — *Cocklorel's Bote* (Wynkyn de Worde 1515) is a story of a clown and a series of rogues in terrible doggerel verse.

p. 104. 'an Italian' — Petrarch
'clerkly' — learnedly

p. 105. 'the music' — the band
'violands' — viols
'pavion' — pavane, a slow, stately dance

p. 106. 'galliard' — a lively dance in triple time

p. 107. 'eftsoons' — afterwards
'bargynet' — probably bergeret, a French shepherd dance
'tintarnell' — dance measure similar to the previous one, but usually without words.
'alla Napolitana' — in the Neopolitan fashion
'tickle' — capricious

p. 108. 'wight' — man
'falcon gent' — the gentlest of falcons will sometimes dally with a scavenger.

'wolves' — Gascoigne's *The Noble Art of Venerie* pp. 204-8 deals with wolves. Here, the foulest wolf is one that has pursued her longest, and thus become foul because of his faithfulness.

p. 109. 'continua oratio' — a complete narration, or 'continual heaping of words' (Richard Sherry, sixteenth-century rhetorician)

p. 110. 'meed' — reward

p. 112. 'common' — an image drawn from the practice of enclosing common grazing land for the sole use of the encloser.

p. 113. 'per misericordiam' — out of pity
'supersedias' — a writ for a stay of execution

p. 114. 'Rugier . . .' — The passage is in *Orlando Furioso* XLIV; it's a letter from Bradamant to Ruggiero assuring him of her faithfulness.
'purvey' — arrange beforehand

p. 115. 'countervail' — equal

p. 116. 'conceits' — thoughts
'sithence' — subsequently
'genealogy of Aeneas' — a reference to Dido and Aeneas in *Aeneid* IV
'express' — squeeze
'cameric' — cambric (fine cotton)
'counterpoint' — quilt

p. 117. 'gear' — business
Cynthia is the moon, Phoebus the sun.
'gare' — perform

p. 118. 'in her despite' — to her disadvantage
'walter' — toss

p. 121. 'subtle' — crafty
'choler' — anger

p. 123. 'sithence' — since

p. 125. 'contray' — contradict

p. 126. 'the pretty bird' — the nightingale. In *The Steel Glass* and *The Complaint of Philomene* an emblem of the poet.

p. 127. 'bezo las manos' — kiss the hands (goodbye)
'allo solito' — as was her custom
'fleering' — impudently laughing

p. 128. 'surquedry' — pride (seen as the root of evil in *The Steel Glass*)

p. 130. 'thriftless' — useless, unsuccessful

The Spoil of Antwerp

p. 131. 'ut supra' — above. Gascoigne has begun his account by describing the earthworks built against the Spaniards, and how easily the crack Spanish troops had overrun them. The extract begins as he changes to first person narrative.
'scarmouch' — skirmish
'use traffic' — are going to business (in the Bourse)
'Helas . . .' — 'Alas, sir, there is no strong point left, and that is the

156

end of this town.' 'Be brave, my friend.'
'Ou est . . .' — 'Where are you running to like cowards? Let's make a stand for the honour of our country.'

p. 132. 'In fine' — in the end

p. 133. 'dalliance' — an oddly playful word in the circumstances
Everstine was in charge of the garrison regiment; the others mentioned on this page came with the reinforcements from the States General, the ruling body of the independent Netherlands.

p. 134. 'Portingal' — Portuguese
'tables of Doomsday' — on the east wall of the Sistine Chapel
'Almains' — Germans

p. 136. 'jetting' — swaggering
'besoigner' — raw recruit

Certain Notes

p. 137. 'quot . . .' — so many men, so many opinions
'Rym, Ram, Ruff' — alliterative verse, as described in the Parson's Prologue in *The Canterbury Tales*.
'aliquid salis' — something of value (literally, salty)
'vix' — scarcely
'tanquam . . .' — just as a continual narration
'& sic . . .' — and so on

p. 139. 'Rhythm' was often thought to be synonymous with 'rhyme' in this period (cf. Puttenham); and 'verse' to be a more dignified term, rather than 'poetry', which was a more general term for artistic 'making' (cf. Sidney, Webbe). Terminology is disturbingly flexible at this early stage of theorizing!

p. 140. 'monosyllables' — Gabriel Harvey comments in the margin of his copy 'Non placet. A great grace and majesty in longer words, so they be current English. Monosyllables are good to make up a hobbling and huddling verse.' He cites Spenser and Sidney to prove his point.

p. 141. 'nequid nimis' — nothing too much
'crambe bis . . .' — cabbage served a second time is deadly (Juvenal, *Satire* VII; about schoolboys repeating their lessons)

p. 142. 'turkeneth' — twists. Subsequent usage has reversed some of Gascoigne's examples.
'ceasures' — now 'caesuras', but Gascoigne characteristically prefers an Englished form.

p. 143. 'Rhythm Royal' — more usually Rhyme Royal
'sonare' — to sing
'sixaines' — ? ought to have six lines, not five
'verlay' — a false etymology

p. 144. 'poulters' — i.e., poulterers, who would sell their eggs in this fashion.

'lammas' — 1 August; 'latter lammas' — a day that will never come (proverbial)

'riding rhyme' — not defined here; subsequent accounts describe it as a loose form of the heroic couplet

INDEX OF FIRST LINES OF POEMS